EDITED FROM THE STUDY BY
TIMOTHY KELLER
ROMANS 1-7
FOR YOU

thegoodbook
COMPANY

Romans 1 – 7 For You

© Timothy Keller, 2014.
Reprinted 2015, 2016, 2017, 2018, 2019, 2022, 2023.

Published by:
The Good Book Company

thegoodbook.com | thegoodbook.co.uk
thegoodbook.com.au | thegoodbook.co.nz | thegoodbook.co.in

ISBN: 9781908762870 | JOB-007624 | Printed in Turkey

Design by André Parker

CONTENTS

SERIES PREFACE

Each volume of the *God's Word For You* series takes you to the heart of a book of the Bible, and applies its truths to your heart.

The central aim of each title is to be:

- Bible centered
- Christ glorifying
- Relevantly applied
- Easily readable

You can use *Romans 1 – 7 For You:*

To read. You can simply read from cover to cover, as a book that explains and explores the themes, encouragements and challenges of this part of Scripture.

To feed. You can work through this book as part of your own personal regular devotions, or use it alongside a sermon or Bible-study series at your church. Each chapter is divided into two shorter sections, with questions for reflection at the end of each.

To lead. You can use this as a resource to help you teach God's word to others, both in small-group and whole-church settings. You'll find tricky verses or concepts explained using ordinary language, and helpful themes and illustrations along with suggested applications.

These books are not commentaries. They assume no understanding of the original Bible languages, nor a high level of biblical knowledge. Verse references are marked in **bold** so that you can refer to them easily. Any words that are used rarely or differently in everyday language outside the church are marked in **gray** when they first appear, and are explained in a glossary toward the back. There, you'll also find details of resources you can use alongside this one, in both personal and church life.

Our prayer is that as you read, you'll be struck not by the contents of this book, but by the book it's helping you open up; and that you'll praise not the author of this book, but the One he is pointing you to.

Carl Laferton, Series Editor

INTRODUCTION TO ROMANS

The letter to the Romans is a book that repeatedly changes the world, by changing people.

One man Romans changed was the English pastor John Stott. Stott's ministry and commitment to evangelism had a great effect on the church in the UK and US, and perhaps particularly throughout the developing world, in the twentieth century. He wrote of his:

> "love-hate relationship with Romans, because of its joyful-painful personal challenges … It was Paul's devastating exposure of universal human sin and guilt in Romans 1:18 – 3:20 which rescued me from that kind of superficial evangelism which is preoccupied only with people's 'felt needs.'"
>
> (*The Message of Romans,* page 10)

Almost five hundred years before Paul's words called Stott to an evangelism which focused on our relationship with God, Romans changed two other men, in a way that would completely transform the church.

Martin Luther was a German monk who had been taught that God required him to live a righteous life in order to be saved. And so he had grown to hate God, for first requiring of him what he could not do, and then for leaving him to fail. Then Luther read and finally grasped the meaning of Romans 1:17—"In the gospel the righteousness of God is revealed—a righteousness that is by faith from first to last" (NIV2011):

> "I labored diligently and anxiously as to how to understand Paul's word … the expression 'the righteousness of God' blocked the way, because I took it to mean that righteousness whereby God is righteous and deals righteously in punishing the unrighteous. Although an impeccable monk, I stood before God as a sinner … therefore I did not love a righteous and angry God, but rather hated and murmured against him …
>
> "Then I grasped that the righteousness of God is that righteousness by which through grace and sheer mercy God justifies us

by faith. Thereupon I felt myself to be reborn and to have gone through open doors into paradise ... I broke through. And as I had formerly hated the expression 'the righteousness of God,' I now began to regard it as my dearest and most comforting word." *(Commentary on the Epistle to the Romans)*

Luther's breakthrough in Romans 1 would lead to the recovery of the gospel in Germany and throughout Europe, and so to the Protestant Reformation. One of the greatest theologians and pastors of that Reformation, the Frenchman John Calvin, who ministered in Geneva, Switzerland, spoke of Romans as his:

"entrance ... to all the most hidden treasures of Scripture ... The subject then of these chapters may be stated thus—man's only righteousness is through the mercy of God in Christ, which being offered by the gospel is apprehended by faith."

(Commentaries on the Epistle of Paul to the Romans, page 16)

Both Luther and Calvin made great use of the writings of an earlier church leader, Augustine, the fourth-century bishop of Hippo (in what is now Algeria). Augustine had a Christian mother, but he turned his back on her faith. He sought truth elsewhere, decided to live however he felt, and fathered a child out of marriage. But while living in Milan, he heard the preaching of Bishop Ambrose, a towering figure in the church. And he found himself unable to shake off what he had heard:

"The tumult of my heart took me out into the garden where no-one could interfere with the burning struggle with myself in which I was engaged ... I was twisting and turning in my chains. Suddenly I heard a voice from the nearby house chanting as if it might be a boy or a girl ... 'Pick up and read, pick up and read.' [I took] the book of the apostle [ie: Romans], opened it and in silence read the first passage on which my eye lit: 'Not in riots or drunken parties, not in eroticism and indecencies, not in strife and rivalry, but put on the Lord Jesus Christ and make no provision for the flesh in its lusts' (13:13-14). I neither wished nor needed to read further. At once, with the last words of this sentence, it was as if a light of relief from all anxiety flooded into my heart. All the shadows of doubt were dispelled."

(*Confessions*, Book VIII, chapters 8 and 12)

So God used the book of Romans to bring to faith the man who may well have been the greatest influence on the church between Paul himself and Luther a millennium later.

What is it about Romans that has proved so life-changing and history-shaping? It is because Romans is about the gospel. Paul was writing to the church in Rome in about AD57 because he wanted them first to understand the gospel, and then to experience the gospel—to know its glorious release. He was likely writing to them during his third missionary journey, quite possibly from Corinth, Greece. They were Christians he had never met, though he hoped to do so soon. They seem to have been a church suffering from tensions between Jewish Christians and Gentile Christians. But though Paul did not have first-hand knowledge of them, he knew what it was they most needed to hear—the gospel.

As both Luther and Calvin describe so powerfully, this "gospel of God" (Romans 1:1) was a declaration about God's righteousness. It was the message that the perfection and holiness of God has been seen in the life and death of Jesus Christ; *and* that this perfection is offered to us, as a free gift, through the life and death of Jesus Christ. That is the "gospel" message of Romans and, as we will see, Paul shows us not only how God in the gospel makes sinners righteous, but also how this most precious gift of God is *enjoyed* in our lives—how it produces deep and massive changes in our behavior and even in our character.

> Paul shows us how received righteousness is *enjoyed* in our lives.

Reading and reflecting on this letter today, we should be prepared to have our hearts shaped and our lives changed by God's gift of righteousness, just as so many others have been. Romans will prompt us to ask: *Have I, like Luther, "broken through" into the freedom and release the gospel brings me, both in terms of my future and in my life right now?*

Romans is perhaps the most written-upon book in the whole of Scripture—its structure and its approach have been the subject of debate throughout the history of the church. In the appendices, I have included a detailed outline structure for the first seven chapters of the letter, to help you see the overall flow and logic of Paul's thinking; several pages on the biblical view of idolatry, which is foundational to Paul's treatment of sin and righteousness in chapters 1 – 3; and a very brief description of and response to the recent debates about who Paul is writing to in Romans, and what he is saying to them.

But this resource is not intended to be an exhaustive, nor final, word! It is not a commentary; it does not go into the depth a commentary would, nor does it interact with historical and recent scholarship. It is an expository guide, opening up the Scripture and suggesting how it applies to us today. My prayer is simply that it will help you to, in Luther's words, "break through": in your understanding of the gospel message; or your experience of the gospel life; or both.

1. INTRODUCING THE GOSPEL

Romans is, at its heart, a letter about the **gospel**. It is written by a man whose life and work revolved around the gospel, showing the difference brought and worked by the gospel. Unsurprisingly, the beginning of the letter is all about the gospel.

Separate for the Gospel

As with all ancient letters, the writer begins by introducing himself. He is "Paul." And first and foremost he is a Christian—"a servant of Christ Jesus" (**v 1**). Servant here is literally slave—*doulos*. Paul, like every Christian, has a Master. He is a man under authority. Second, Paul has been "called to be an apostle" (**v 1**). He is an *apostolos*—a "sent one." This is not a job Paul selected himself for, or even applied for. He was "called" into it—he was **commissioned** and taught directly by the risen Jesus himself (see Acts 9:1-19). He has direct authority from Christ to teach. What he writes is Scripture. What follows is true.

But why did the Lord call Paul to be his apostle? So that he would be "set apart for the gospel of God" (Romans **1:1**). The word translated "set apart" means "separated," to be moved away and apart from everything else. Paul was set apart to spread the gospel, to pursue this one overriding aim. This is what Paul will "slave" for all his life; but it is also, as we will see (v 9, 11, 15), what he will rejoice in through

---

* All Romans verse references being looked at in each chapter are in **bold**.
† Words in **gray** are defined in the Glossary (page 173).

all his life. To Paul, this gospel is so great that he is willing to separate himself from *anything*—wealth, health, acclaim, friends, safety and so on—in order to be faithful to his calling.

The Gospel: Who, not What

What is this "gospel" for which Paul is willing to glory in being a slave? What gospel would make Paul happy to lose everything in order to share it? First, it is worth reflecting on the word itself. "Gospel"—*euangeloi*—is literally "good herald." In the first century, if on a far-flung battlefield an emperor won a great victory which secured his peace and established his authority, he would send heralds—*angeloi*—to declare his victory, peace and authority. Put most simply, the gospel is an announcement—a declaration. The gospel is not advice to be followed; it is news, good (*eu*) news about what has been done.

The apostle Paul is the herald of this announcement. It is a good reminder that the gospel is not Paul's; it did not originate with him and he did not claim the authority to craft it. Rather, it is "of God" (**v 1**). We, like Paul, are not at liberty to reshape it to sound more appealing in our day, nor to domesticate it to be more comfortable for our lives.

Neither is the gospel new; rather, God "promised it beforehand through his prophets in the Holy Scriptures" (**v 2**). The Old Testament is all about it. All the "Scriptures" point forward to this announcement. They are the scaffold on which Paul stands as God's herald. Every page that God wrote before outlines what he has now declared in full color.

> The gospel is about a person, not a concept; about him, not us.

The gospel's content is "his Son" (**v 3**). The gospel centers on Jesus. It is about a person, not a concept; it is about him, not us. We never grasp the gospel until we understand that it is not fundamentally a message about our lives, dreams, or hopes. The gospel speaks about, and transforms, all of those things, but only because it isn't about us. It is a declaration about God's Son, the man Jesus. This Son was:

- fully human: "as to his human nature" (**v 3**).

- the one who fulfilled the promises of Scripture: he was "a descendant of David" (**v 3**), the king of Israel a millennium before. God had promised David that from his family God would produce the ultimate, final, universal King—the Christ (see 2 Samuel 7:11b-16). And David's own life—his rule, suffering and glory—in many ways foreshadowed that of his greater descendant (see Psalms 2; 22; 110).

- divine: the Son was "declared with power to be the Son of God, by his resurrection from the dead" (Romans **1:4**). Paul is not saying that Jesus only became God's Son when he was raised from the grave. Rather, he is outlining two great truths about the resurrection. First, the empty tomb is the great declaration of who Jesus is. His resurrection removes all doubt that he is the Son of God. Second, his resurrection and **ascension** were his path to his rightful place; to his rule at God's right hand (Ephesians 1:19b-22), sitting at "the highest place," given "the name that is above every name, that at the name of Jesus every knee should bow" (Philippians 2:9-10). God's Son had humbly become a man, tasted poverty, endured rejection and suffered a powerless death. The resurrection is where we see not only that he is the Son of God, but that he is now the Son of God "*in power.*"

Not until the end of Romans **1:4** does Paul actually name God's Son: "Jesus Christ our Lord." God's Son is Jesus, the Greek version of the Hebrew name *Yeshua/Joshua*—"God will save," the fulfiller of all God "promised beforehand" (**v 2**). He is Christ, the anointed man whom God has appointed to rule his people. And he is our Lord, God himself. The gospel is both a declaration of Jesus' perfect rule, and an invitation to come under that perfect rule, to make him "*our* Lord."

Faith-fueled Obedience

This is the gospel Paul announces. He has "received **grace** and apostleship" (**v 5**—ie: both his job as apostle, and the power to accomplish it, grace). And his specific role is "to call people from among all the **Gentiles**." The gospel is for God's ancient people, the Jews—but it is not only for them. God has commissioned Paul to take the message of his Son to those who are not Jews. He is God's "chosen instrument to carry my name before the Gentiles and their kings and before the people of Israel" (Acts 9:15).

And what is the gospel call? To obey Christ and trust Christ—to live by "the obedience that comes from faith" (Romans **1:5**). What does this mean? The rest of the book of Romans will explain it! But it is worth highlighting two things here.

First, it does *not* mean that Paul is teaching the Gentiles that, to be saved, they must both have **faith** and do obedience, as though both are necessary grounds of being right with God. This is an obedience that comes from faith—that springs from a wholehearted trust in Jesus, God's Son. Obedience flows out of faith; it is a consequence of saving faith, not a second condition for salvation.

But second, it *does* mean that true faith in our hearts brings obedience in our lives. Why? Because the gospel is the declaration that Jesus is the promised King, the risen and powerful Son of God, who now invites us in, to enjoy the blessings of his rule. Again, we will see much more of why we need to be invited, how this invitation is possible, and how wonderful Jesus' rule is, in the rest of Paul's letter. Here, the point is that real "faith" is faith in a divine King, to whom we owe our obedience and of whom we (like Paul) are servants. There *will* be a joyful obedience that flows from truly trusting this King. As the great sixteenth-century **Reformer** Martin Luther put it: "We are saved by faith

> Real faith is faith in a divine King, to whom we owe our joyful obedience.

alone, but the faith that saves is never alone." It brings about grateful, joyful, trusting obedience.

Why Paul Went to Rome

This life of faith and faith-fuelled obedience encompasses "you also," the church in Rome, Paul says. In **verses 6-7**, he describes these Christians in four wonderful ways. First, they have been "called to belong to Jesus Christ." Second, they are "loved by God." Third, they are "called to be saints"—literally, pure ones or set-apart ones. Fourth, they enjoy "grace and peace … from God our Father and from the Lord Jesus Christ."

Paul is moved to "thank my God through Jesus Christ for all of you, because your faith is being reported all over the world" (**v 8**). Paul himself has never been to this church, but he has heard a lot about it. He has been praying for them (**v 9-10**); and he has been praying that now he might be able to come to Rome in person (**v 10**).

Why does Paul want to visit this church, which is already clearly living out an obedience which comes from faith, and for whom he can thank God and pray from afar? "So that I may impart to you some spiritual gift to make you strong" (**v 11**). He wants to use his abilities of preaching and pastoring so that they can be encouraged in their faith (**v 12**). There is a surprise here. The great apostle does not want to visit simply so he can encourage them. He will visit so that they can encourage him, too—"that you *and* I may be *mutually* encouraged *by each other's* faith" (**v 12**).

This is striking! Since Paul sought out encouragement from other believers, and since if Paul sought that encouragement in the faith of other believers, how much more should we?! **Verses 11-12** begin to show us part of what the obedience that comes through faith is; it is obeying Christ by having the humility to serve, and be served by, his people. **Verse 11** teaches us to use whatever gifts the Lord has graciously given us to make others stronger in their faith. **Verse 12** teaches us to allow others to use the faith and gifts the Lord has given them to build us up. We should never leave our church meetings, having spent time surrounded by beloved, distinctive people of faith, without feeling encouraged!

How can we know that encouragement in reality, Sunday by Sunday and week by week as we meet together, though? By remembering that God has declared that Jesus is his Son, raised with power to rule in power, and that by faith in him we enjoy grace from him and peace with him. When we spend time with other believers, we are spending time with those who say: *This is true* and: *This is wonderful* to that declaration. We can see faith, and the obedience that flows from it, all around us. We can see others using their gifts for others, and we can use ours for them. That is what encourages and strengthens us.

Questions for reflection

1. What is missing from the gospel you believe in if you forget or downplay the truth that God's Son is "Jesus"… or "Christ"… or "Lord"? Do you ever downplay one or other of these in how you think and live?

2. Where can you see the "obedience that comes from faith" in your own life?

3. What difference would it make if you went to church next Sunday consciously seeking to encourage others? Do you allow the faith and words of others to encourage you?

PART TWO

Harvest Time in Rome

Paul has a second purpose for visiting Rome, though it is linked to the first of encouraging and being encouraged. He has "planned many times to come to you … in order that I might have a harvest among you, just as I have had among the other Gentiles" (**v 13**).

This "harvest" Likely has two aspects. Paul is hoping for a harvest *within* the Roman church; what Jesus pictured when he talked of people who had heard and accepted the word producing "a crop— thirty, sixty or even a hundred times what was sown" (Mark 4:20). But the next verses show that Paul also desires to reap a crop *outside* the church; what Jesus was talking of when he said to his followers: "The harvest is plentiful but the workers are few. Ask the Lord of the harvest, therefore, to send out workers into his harvest field" (Matthew 9:37-38). Paul is coming to Rome both to encourage and to **evangelize**.

Paul sees himself as "obligated," to Greeks and non-Greeks, to wise and foolish; to everyone, no matter their ethnic background or intellectual capabilities (Romans **1:14**). "Obligated" can also be rendered "indebted." Yet Paul has never met the Roman church, far less the greater population of Rome. So in what sense is he in debt to them? It is illustrative to think about how I can be in debt to you. First, you may have lent me $100—and I am in debt to you until I pay it back. But second, someone else may have given me $100 to pass on to you—and I am in debt to you until I hand it on. It is in this second sense that Paul is "obligated" to everyone, everywhere. God has shared the gospel with him. But God has also commissioned him to declare it to others. So Paul owes people the gospel.

Setting **verse 14** alongside verse 5 provides us with Paul's motivation for his witness. First, it is "for his name's sake" (v 5). The gospel declares that Jesus is the powerful, saving King. His status demands honor. His actions in dying and rising deserve honor. And he is honored as he is recognized as "our Lord." It is for Jesus' sake that Paul tells people the gospel.

But second, it is also for people's sake. We will see who needs the gospel, and why, in the next three chapters of this book. But **verse 14** gives us the sense of Paul's burning desire to settle his debt by passing on the message of the gospel which God gave to him. It is his love and regard for Jesus, and his love and regard for people, which are "why I am so eager to preach the gospel also to you who are at Rome" (**v 15**). Everyone needs the gospel, both the "you" inside the church and the "you" who are yet outside it. The gospel is the way people are called to faith, and the way people grow in faith.

We do not have Paul's specific commission as apostle to the Gentiles. But we are still commissioned by the Lord to: "go and make disciples of all nations, baptizing them in the name of the Father and of the Son and of the Holy Spirit, and teaching them to obey everything I have commanded you" (Matthew 28:19-20). Calling people to the "obedience that comes from faith" is a commission given to all believers, because: "all authority in heaven and on earth has been given to [Jesus]. Therefore go..." (v 18-19).

Eager or Ashamed?

But in every age, it is possible to be "ashamed of the gospel" (Romans **1:16**), instead of eager to share it. The word translated "ashamed" also means "offended." How is the gospel offensive?

1. The gospel, by telling us that our salvation is free and undeserved, is really insulting! It tells us that we are such spiritual failures that the only way to gain salvation is for it to be a complete gift. This offends moral and religious people who think their decency gives them an advantage over less moral people.

2. The gospel is also really insulting by telling us that Jesus died for us. It tells us that we are so wicked that only the death of the Son

of God could save us. This offends the modern cult of self-expression and the popular belief in the innate goodness of humanity.

3. The gospel, by telling us that trying to be good and spiritual isn't enough, thereby insists that no "good" person will be saved, but only those who come to God through Jesus. This offends the modern notion that any nice person anywhere can find God "in his own way." We don't like losing our **autonomy**.

4. The gospel tells us that our salvation was accomplished by Jesus' suffering and serving (not conquering and destroying), and that following him means to suffer and serve with him. This offends people who want salvation to be an easy life; it also offends people who want their lives to be safe and comfortable.

I am not Ashamed Because...

Yet Paul is *not* ashamed of the shameful gospel. In **verses 16-17**, we find Paul's nutshell summary of the gospel—his central thesis statement out of which flows the rest of the letter.

First, he is not ashamed of the gospel because "it is the power of God" (**v 16**). Paul is often fond of contrasting "mere" words with power (see, for instance, 1 Corinthians 4:20). Paul is saying that the gospel is not merely a concept or a philosophy. In the gospel, words and power come together. The message of the gospel is what God has done and will do for us. Paul says that the gospel is therefore a power. He doesn't say it brings power or has power, but that it actually *is* power. The gospel message is actually the power of God in verbal,

> The gospel message is the power of God in verbal form.

cognitive form. It lifts people up; it transforms and changes things. When it is outlined and explained, or reflected upon, its power is released.

Theodoret, a Syrian bishop in the fifth century, likened the gospel to a pepper: "A pepper outwardly seems to be cold … but the person who crunches it between the teeth experiences the sensation of burning fire." In the same way, he goes on, the gospel can appear at first like an interesting theory or philosophy. But if we take it in personally, we find it full of power.

What does its power *do*? It is the power of God "unto salvation" (Romans **1:16**, KJV). The gospel's power is seen in its ability to completely change minds, hearts, life orientation, our understanding of everything that happens, the way people relate to one another, and so on. Most of all, it is powerful because it does what no other power on earth can do: it can save us, reconcile us to God, and guarantee us a place in the **kingdom of God** forever.

All that is required to know this salvation is belief: it is offered to "everyone who believes" (**v 16**). Here we have the first explicit statement that the only way to receive the gospel and its power is through faith. Faith is thus the channel or connection to the power of the gospel, just as a light switch is the channel or connection between a light bulb and an electrical source.

Notice that Paul says that the gospel's power is boundless and boundaried at the same time. He says it is to *everyone*. It came to the Jew first, through Jesus, but it is for the Gentile as well—everyone and anyone. Yet he also sets a limit on it. It is for everyone *who believes*.

Righteousness Revealed

What is it about the gospel which makes it so powerful, which gives it this life-remolding quality? Because—"for"—"in the gospel a righteousness from God is revealed" (**v 17**). The gospel is about the Son— but here we see the achievement of the gospel, that in it "a righteousness from God is revealed."

We can get a pretty good handle on "righteousness" by thinking about the English word. What does it mean to be "right" with your company, your government or another person? It is a positional word—it means to have a good or right standing, to have no debts or liabilities that you owe the other person or organization. You are acceptable to the other party because your record has nothing on it to jeopardize the relationship. The other party has nothing against you.

The "righteousness of God" could refer to God's righteous character. He is perfectly good and holy. He is without fault or blame. But Paul is speaking here of a righteousness *from* God (as the NIV makes clear). This is an unparalleled claim, as the word "revealed" shows— no one would ever know of it, find it, or guess it, unless God showed it through his word. Right standing is received from God, offered to us by his Son.

This is what the rather complex wording in the middle of **verse 17** is saying. The NIV translates it "by faith from first to last," on which reading Paul is simply saying that righteousness is received through faith, and always only received by faith. We do not become righteous by faith and then maintain it through our own goodness. But the ESV has a more accurate translation: righteousness is "from faith for faith," in which case the teaching is, as John Stott explains:

> We do not become righteous by faith and then maintain it through our own goodness.

"God's faithfulness [to His promises, and in the life and death of Jesus Christ] always comes first, and ours is never other than a response."   (*The Message of Romans*, page 64)

It is important to realize how much more is promised here than mere forgiveness. Many people think Jesus died merely to forgive us. Our sins were laid on him, and we are pardoned when we believe in him. That is true, but that is only half of Christian salvation. If that were all Jesus did, we would then only receive a new "wiped clean" slate. It would be up to us to add credit or merit to our account. But here Paul tells us that we have been given righteousness, rather than merely declared not guilty.

Jesus' salvation is not only like receiving a pardon and release from death row and prison. Then we'd be free, but on our own, left to make our own way in the world, thrown back on our own efforts if we're to make anything of ourselves. But in the gospel, we discover that Jesus has taken us off death row and then has hung around our neck the Congressional Medal of Honor. We are received and welcomed as heroes, as if we had accomplished extraordinary deeds.

How To Not Live By Faith

This, Paul says, is always how righteousness has been received (he will go into more detail on this theme in chapter 4). "As it is written," he says in **verse 17**, quoting Habakkuk 2:4: "The righteous will live by faith." In thinking through what Paul means here, perhaps it is most helpful to think about how people (including Christians) might *not* live by faith. At the root of each and every sin, and each and every problem, is unbelief and a rejection of the gospel. People who are immoral and people who are moral both reject the gospel when they try to be their own savior.

1. When **licentious** people reject religion and God, their rebellion is really a refusal to believe the gospel—the message that they are so sinful, only Jesus can be their Savior.

2. When moralistic people pick up religion and morality and become either anxious (because they are aware they can never live up to the standards) or proud (because they think they have), their anxiety and/or pride is really a refusal to believe the gospel—the message that they are so sinful, only Jesus can be their Savior.

3. When Christian people sin, it always involves forgetting that they cannot save themselves; only Jesus can. When we are bitter, it is because we have forgotten that we are already totally saved by grace alone—so how can we withhold grace? When we are

overworking out of fear of failure or depressed because we have failed, it is because we have forgotten that we cannot earn our own righteousness, but that in God's eyes we are already righteous.

The gospel will always cause offense, because it reveals us as having a need that we cannot meet. So we will always be tempted to be ashamed of it. We need to remember that it is the power of God. We need to remember it reveals God's righteousness, and is the way we receive his righteousness. This is what fundamentally reverses our attitude to sharing the gospel. The opposite of being ashamed is not willingness; it is eagerness. We become eager when we know the truth, the wonder and the power of the gospel so deeply that we herald it not because we know we *ought* to, or because we feel we *have* to, but because we want to and love to, "for his name's sake."

Questions for reflection

1. Meditate on how Jesus demands and deserves recognition and respect. How will this motivate you to talk about him this week?

2. In what situations do you find yourself being ashamed of the gospel? How could verses 16-17 turn that to eagerness next time?

3. Think about a sin you struggle with. How are you rejecting the gospel when you sin in that way? How will believing the gospel transform the next struggle you face?

2. THE PAGANS NEED THE GOSPEL

Paul's nutshell outline in verses 16-17 raises a question: Why *must* the righteous live by faith? Why is a *received* righteousness the only way to be in right standing with God? Paul will spend from 1:18 to 3:20 showing us why we need God to give us righteousness—why we cannot earn, deserve or attain it ourselves. It will present us with a dark picture of humanity. Yet it is the backdrop on which the bright jewel of the gospel shines all the brighter.

Anger Revealed

Verse 18 begins "For" (ESV). So verse 18 flows out of verses 16-17; Paul is showing us that the gospel is necessary not simply to make me happy, but because there is such a thing as "the wrath of God" that I face. Paul's confidence, joy and passion for the gospel rest on the assumption that all human beings are, apart from the gospel, under God's wrath. If you don't understand or believe in the wrath of God, the gospel will not thrill, empower or move you.

God's wrath—his settled, fair, right anger—is, Paul says, a present reality. It "*is being* revealed" (**v 18**). He does not say: *The wrath of God will be revealed*. It is seen *now*, today. This prompts two questions: *Why is it being revealed?* and *How is it being revealed?* The rest of the chapter gives his answers.

Suppression

What draws God's anger is "godlessness and wickedness." The first speaks to a disregard of God's rights, a destruction of our vertical relationship with him. The second refers to a disregard of human rights to love, truth, justice etc, a destruction of horizontal relationships with those around us. It is a breaking of what Jesus said were the greatest two commandments: to love God, and to love our neighbor (Mark 12:29-31).

Paul immediately anticipates the objection that people do not know any better. How can God hold someone accountable for not knowing a God they have never heard of? But in fact, everyone knows better, because they do know the truth, and suppress it. Romans **1:21** goes so far as to say that all human beings, everywhere and in all times, "knew God." They knew because God has made himself "plain to them ... since [and in] the creation of the world" (**v 19-20**). Creation shows us that there is a God of "eternal power and divine nature." We all know, regardless of what we tell ourselves, that there is a Creator, on whom we are utterly dependent and to whom we are completely accountable. We cannot know everything about God from creation—his love and mercy, for instance—but we can, and do, deduce that whoever created all this must be a being of unimaginable greatness. And then we suppress that truth.

> We all know there is a Creator, on whom we are dependent and to whom we are accountable.

This is a counter-cultural teaching. Christians, to whom God's Spirit has shown the truth about the Creator, are often accused of being repressed—not truly being themselves or opening themselves up to the world as it really is. But Paul says that, naturally, we are all repressed, for as long as we hold down the truth that there is a Creator God. For as long as we suppress that truth, we will never understand who we are, or why the world is as it is. It is not acknowledging the Creator's right to be Ruler that is repressive; rather, it is the self-suppression of living in denial of that truth.

Everyone Worships Something

So, Paul says, "men are without excuse." Every human knows God, but no human glorifies God or gives thanks to him (**v 21**). This sounds as though God's wrath comes in response to bad manners: forgetting to say "thank you!" But Paul is saying that we are plagiarists. We take what God has made, and pass it off as our own. We don't acknowledge our dependence on our Creator, but claim to be independent. We prefer the illusion that we can call the shots and decide what is right and wrong to the reality that creation speaks to us of. We are not grateful because we don't accept what he has done for us and around us.

What happens when people refuse to acknowledge and depend on God as God? We do not stop worshiping. We simply change the object of our worship. Paul says that people "exchanged the glory of the immortal God for images made to look like mortal man and birds and animals and reptiles" (**v 23**). We see this exchange again in verses **25, 26** and (implicitly) **27**. Instead of worshiping the true God, people "worshiped and served created things rather than the Creator" (**v 25**).

We must worship *something*. We were created to worship the Creator, so if we reject him, we will worship something else. We are "tellic" creatures—purposed people; we have to live for something. There has to be something which captures our imagination and our allegiance, which is the resting place of our deepest hopes and which we look to to calm our deepest fears. Whatever that thing is, we worship it, and so we serve it. It becomes our bottom line, the thing we cannot live without, defining and validating everything we do.

Because God created the world "very good" (Genesis 1:31), all created things have good in them. We are right to find them admirable and to enjoy them. The problem comes from giving any created thing inordinate affection—the ultimate affection, which only God deserves and has the right to demand. Paul is saying that the human heart loves to make a good thing into its god thing.

This exchange in our worship and service undoes the created order. Humans are uniquely made in the image of God, made to relate to him in his world and reflect his nature and goodness to the world (Genesis 1:26-29). In Romans **1:23**, humanity turns its back on God and turns to bowing down to created things. We do not worship what is immortal; we worship what is made. Put another way, we do not worship the Creator; we worship the created (**v 25**).

> We do not worship what is immortal; we worship what is made.

From God's perspective, this is the behavior of "fools" (**v 22**). How has this happened? Because, Paul says in a few very revealing words in **verse 21**, in refusing to treat God as God, and live in dependence on and gratitude to him, "their thinking became futile and their foolish hearts were darkened." In order to suppress the truth that there is a Creator, people engage in **non-sequiturs** and irrational leaps. Since the fundamental truth about God is being held down and ignored, life cannot be lived in a consistent way.

Take morality, for instance. If there is no God who has the right to say what is right and wrong, how are we to find moral absolutes? It is very arrogant to say: *This is wrong because I say it is.* But no one in the end wants to say: *This is wrong because society says it is.* After all, most of American (and European) society thought slavery wasn't wrong 300 years ago. If morality is defined by majority, slavery was not wrong back then! If there is no God, there is nowhere to locate the authority to give a moral absolute. But no one lives as though there is no right and wrong (they may say they do, but they cry for justice when they or a loved one is "wronged").

The twentieth-century Christian philosopher and minister Greg Bahnsen put it brilliantly in a debate (as well as in his book *Presuppositional Apologetics*):

"Imagine a person who comes in here tonight and argues 'no air exists' but continues to breathe air while he argues. Now intellectually, atheists continue to breathe—they continue to use reason and draw scientific conclusions [which assumes an orderly universe], to make moral judgments [which assumes absolute values]—but the atheistic view of things would in theory make such 'breathing' impossible. They are breathing God's air all the time they are arguing against him."

The Wrath of Giving us What we Want

Paul has built a substantial case for the rightness and deservedness of God's anger—he will go on doing so in verses 26-32. But in **verse 24**, we discover *how* God's wrath is being revealed in the present.

God's judgment on godlessness and wickedness is to give us what we want. He "gave them over in the sinful desires of their hearts." The things we serve will not free us; rather, they control us. We *have* to have them. And, since our hearts were made to be centered on God, since he is the only true provider of satisfaction and significance, they do not satisfy—we always feel we need more, or something else. The tragedy of humanity is that we strive for and fail to find what we could simply receive and enjoy. We suppress the truth which would free and satisfy us.

The word that the NIV translates "sinful desires" and the ESV renders "lusts" is *epithumia*. Literally, it means "over-desire," an all-controlling drive and longing. This is revealing. The main problem of our heart is not so much desires for bad things, but our over-desires for good things, our turning of created, good things into gods, objects of our worship and service.

And the worst thing that can happen to us is that we are given what our hearts over-desire. Take a man who worships his career. He serves it as what will make him "a somebody." It drives him, and it dominates his life—everything else is fitted around it. The worst thing that can happen to him is promotion! It allows him to continue to think that he can find blessing in his over-desires. It convinces him that this is "real life." It enables him to forget the wreckage he is making of his marriage, his family, his friendships, in order to pursue his god.

Oscar Wilde summed it up well: "When the gods wish to punish us, they answer our prayers." This is the wrath of God: to give us what we want too much, to give us over to the pursuit of the things we have put in place of him. The worst thing God can do to human beings in the present is to let them reach their idolatrous goals. His judgment is to give us over to the destructive power of idolatry, and of evil. When we sin, it sets up stresses and strains in the fabric of the order that God created. Instead of us finding blessing, our sin causes breakdowns spiritually, psychologically, socially and physically.

> God allows us to walk through the door we have chosen.

The great tragedy is that we choose this for ourselves. God allows us to walk through the door we have chosen.

The Freedom of Praise

Is there any escape, any way back? We will need to wait for Romans chapter 3 to see once more the dazzling jewel of the gospel. But **verse 25** does give us a clue. "The Creator [should be] forever praised. Amen." The way out is to stop suppressing the truth, and praise God as God—to depend on him and accept his right to rule over us; to desire him more than we desire anything that he has made.

Where do we find the motivation, the freedom and the power to do this? It is only discovered in the gospel, where we find that, godless and wicked though we naturally are, in Christ we are loved and accepted and blessed. It is as we understand the gospel—as we appreciate that our Lord is also our Savior—that we are led to find freedom in praising the Creator. How do we know we have understood and received that gospel? When the thing we are most looking forward to in eternity is praising him forever.

Questions for reflection

1. Do you see the truths of these verses in your own life before you were a Christian? Do you see fragments of this attitude in your life now?

2. How does understanding the inconsistency caused by truth-suppression help us to speak to nonbelievers about the Christian faith?

3. How, and how often, will you spend time simply giving glory and thanks to God for your life in his world this week?

PART TWO

Until **verse 24**, Paul has been focusing on humanity's vertical relationship with our Creator. We do know God's existence, his power and divinity. We should glorify him by living in dependent gratitude. Instead, we suppress the truth and worship created things, turning God-made good things into gods we have made for ourselves.

But, ever since Genesis 3, it has been clear that in God's world, subverting our relationship with God has an effect on our relationships with each other, and with the creation. Damaging our vertical relationship damages our horizontal relationships. God has created a world where living under his rule and enjoying his blessing is the way in which we, in turn, rule the world in a way which blesses it (Genesis 1:28). When we worship an idol in his place, he is no longer the one thing we have to have in life; something else is. It rules us; and ultimately we will do anything—however destructive to ourselves or others—to have it, increase it, or keep it.

It is to the horizontal effects of exchanging God for an idol that Paul now turns.

Paul and Homosexuality

Romans **1:26-27** is one of the more controversial passages in Scripture. It is the longest passage in the Bible on homosexuality.

Recently, many have attempted to suggest that the traditional understanding of these verses is mistaken; that this refers to people who act against their *own* nature; or that it refers only to promiscuous homosexual sex, and not to long-term settled relationships. But "unnatural relations" (**v 26, 27**) is literally "against nature"—*para phusin*. This means that homosexuality is a violation of the created nature God gave us. And there is nothing here to suggest that Paul only has some kinds of homosexual acts in mind. As a cultured and traveled Roman citizen, Paul would have been very familiar with long-term, stable, loving relationships between same-sex couples. That does not stop him from identifying them as not the Creator's intention for human flourishing.

Paul is saying: *Here is a way in which God has, in his wrath, given humans over to their over-desires, to experience the consequences.* (This is how the end of **verse 27** should be understood—the "due penalty" is simply reaping the results of idol-worship. "Due penalty" is a punishment not restricted to homosexuality.) The Bible is clear, both in the Old and New Testaments, that active homosexual sex as a settled, unrepentant pattern of behavior is indicative of an attitude of rejection of Jesus' lordship, and leaves people outside his kingdom (see 1 Corinthians 6:9-10), though never outside his reach (v 11).

Two observations need to be made here. First, in Romans 1 Paul chooses to highlight first all sex outside marriage (**Romans 1:24**), and then more specifically homosexual sex (**v 26-27**), as an over-desire which both results in, and is an outworking of, God's "giving over" wrath. It is an unavoidable fact that the Bible says that homosexuality is a sin. But elsewhere in his letters, Paul mentions other examples of idolatrous behavior. So in Colossians 3:5, Paul identifies "greed, *which is idolatry.*" Greed—that is, the constant desire and destructive drive for more—is as indicative of idol-worship as sexual immorality.

> Greed is as indicative of idol-worship as sexual immorality.

And then in Galatians 4:8-9, he says something very surprising. Speaking to Christians who had been **pagans** before they had come to trust Christ, and who now are being tempted to take on all the Jewish religious laws as a means to be saved, he says: "You were slaves to those who by nature are not gods [which is uncontroversial—they had been pagans] … how is it that you are turning back to those weak and miserable principles? Do you wish to be enslaved by them all over again?"

What is the point? That Paul teaches that seeking blessing and salvation through biblical morality is just as much idolatry—setting up a ruler and savior other than God—as greed, or homosexuality. We will worship what we think we need to fulfill ourselves, to give us "life." If we do not worship God, we will worship something else—sexual gratification, increasing our possessions, keeping rules; and none of these are more (or less) serious than the others.

So the second necessary observation is that, while homosexuality *is* a sin, it is *a* sin—not *the worst* sin. All sexual immorality is sinful (Romans **1:24**); and Paul is about to list out other sins in **verses 29-31**, which he calls "wickedness"—acts which issue from our rejection of the truth about God, and damage our horizontal relationships, and which deservedly bring God's wrath (v 18).

This means that there are two ways to misunderstand—or ignore—God's word at this point:

■ Some churches, in an effort to appear relevant to the culture, and to seem loving and welcoming to homosexual people, have downplayed or denied the clear teaching of Scripture on homosexuality, such as **verses 26-27**. We might call this the "liberal" approach.

■ Other churches take what the Bible says on homosexuality very seriously, but in a very self-righteous way. They see homosexuality as *the* sin that matters (or if they do not, they speak and live as though it is). They do not seek to love or welcome gay people at all. They may seek to love and get alongside their Hindu neighbors or friends who are committing adultery, but not homosexual people. We might characterize this as a "conservative" approach.

Paul isn't doing either. He is clear that homosexuality is (literally) a "shameful over-desire" (**v 26**). But remember, he then lists a lot of other sins which, for many of us, strike a lot closer to home—envy, or gossiping, or disobedience, or disloyalty (**v 29-30**). And people who do these things are the same people among whom he wants to have a gospel harvest! Paul is not saying: *It doesn't matter what you do; God doesn't mind as long as you're happy*. But he is also not saying:

What you do matters so much that I don't want to love you or witness to you, because you are beyond the gospel.

How do you know you are, deep down, saying the latter? Because you see homosexual acts as a "perversion," but you don't think of deceit or boasting as "depraved" (**v 28**). We only grasp the gospel when we understand, as Paul did, that *we* are the worst sinner we know (1 Timothy 1:15)—and that if Jesus came to die for us, there is no one that he would not die for. This sets us free to obey Jesus in loving our neighbor; and to be able to accept Jesus' definition of neighbor as being the person who our culture (church or secular) tells us is, or should be, beyond help (Luke 10:25-37).

Seeing Ourselves in Romans One

Romans **1:28-32** is unsettling because, as we've already seen, all of us find ourselves there, one way or another. This is not an exhaustive list of the outworkings of idolatry—of not thinking it "worthwhile to retain the knowledge of God" (**v 28**)—but it is a wide-ranging one. Here we have economic disorder ("greed," **v 29**); social disorder ("murder, strife, deceit and malice," **v 29**); family breakdown ("they disobey their parents," **v 30**); relational breakdown ("senseless, faithless, heartless, ruthless," **v 31**). This is what theologians call the doctrine of total depravity: while not everything we do is always completely sinful, nothing we do is completely untouched by sin.

What does Paul mean at the beginning of **verse 32**, when he says that people know "that those who do such things deserve death"? Likely, he is referring to our consciences. Almost every person, in every single society, has understood that there is right and wrong. We may decide we have the right to define them, but we agree on the category. We know there are things which deserve punishment.

And yet, Paul says, humans decide to "approve of those who practice them" (**v 32**). He has in view people who promote and encourage idolatry. It is easier to see how others do this, and harder to see it in ourselves. But it is worth asking: *Do I ever encourage my children to* make idols of exam results? How might I nod sympathetically at some-one's envy? Have I allowed gossip to go on around me unchallenged?

Three Right Responses

How should God's people respond to these verses, and the dark view of humanity they give us? First, we will recognize that here is a picture which maps onto the reality of the world. All systems of thought must account both for the awesomeness of the cosmos, and the goodness of which humanity is capable; and for the brokenness of the world, our societies, and our lives and relationships. Why is there so much beauty; why is it so flawed? Paul's answer is simple: *God*. There is a God who made it all, and made us in his image, to know and reflect his character. And that same God has, in wrath, given us what we have chosen: life without him, worshiping things which cannot satisfy. In the beauty of the world, we are to see God's existence. In the bro-kenness of the world, we are to see God's justice. As we do, we run back to the place where we see God's mercy: the cross.

Second, we will not shake our heads and roll our eyes self-right-eously at what "they" are like. Paul has referred to "they" throughout these verses. He is talking about Gentile society; and he knows that a self-righteous, religious Jew will hear his words and say: *You're ab-solutely right, Paul. These irreligious people are deserving of God's anger. And I'm glad you picked on homosexuality—as a Jew, that's a sin that I consider particularly reprehen-sible. I'm so glad I'm not like them.*

> The function of these verses is to draw out any self-righteous pride in us.

The function of these verses is to draw out any self-righteous pride in us; any feeling of satisfaction that: *They are wicked; and I am not like them.* As we will see, Paul will next turn to confront that religious, moral man: "You, therefore, have no excuse, you who pass judgment on someone else, for at whatever point you judge the other, you are condemning yourself" (2:1). Self-righteousness is always self-condemnatory. And self-righteousness is the preserve of the moralist.

Rather, and third, we are to read these verses in light of 1:16-17, knowing that we do not need to fear God's wrath because we have received his righteousness. This gives us both the humility and the freedom to ask: *What idols could be, or are already, jostling for position with my Creator in my heart and life?* This passage prompts us to look for places where we are envious, slanderous, disloyal, lusting, and so on. These things are the indication that we are worshiping an idol; that something other than God has become our functional master. And so we need to ask: *What would it look like to depend on my Creator in this area? How would I love and feel and live differently if I praised my Creator at that point, rather than serving a created thing?* That is the way to turn our *epithumia*, our over-desires, into simple enjoyment; not serving as slaves what God has made, but appreciating them in praise of God in his world.

Questions for reflection

1. Which "over-desires" do you most struggle with yourself? Do any of the sins Paul mentions in verses 26-27 and 29-31 describe you?

2. How can you ensure that the sinfulness of the world drives you not to self-righteousness, but to the cross of mercy?

3. Are there any ways in which these verses have drawn out self-righteousness in your heart?

3. THE RELIGIOUS NEED THE GOSPEL (PART ONE)

In chapter 1, Paul has shown how the pagan Gentile world has rejected God, and has been given over to the godlessness and wickedness it has chosen. Paul's critique of the pagan world and lifestyle would have been roundly supported by any Jewish person listening to him. But they would have assumed that they were exempt from his condemnation; they were **law**-keeping Jews.

And that is exactly how religious people would listen to Romans 1:18-32 today. They would say: *Yes, of course God's wrath lies on the immoral, the pagan, the one who lives a life of debauchery. But we have the word of God, and live by that. We are not condemned.* Religious people will seem to agree with Paul about Romans 1:18-32... and will be missing the whole point.

So **2:1** comes as a bucket of cold water to the religious person. It is an absolute masterstroke. Paul turns to the person who has been sitting and listening to his exposé of pagan lifestyles in chapter 1, and feeling pleased that they are not like "them." Paul says: *You do the same things! Whenever you judge a non-religious person, you are judging yourself!* It turns out that the end of chapter 1 is written to expose the idols of the religious person as much as those of the irreligious person.

> 2:1 comes as a bucket of cold water to the religious person.

Judging Yourself

No one truly lives up to their own standards. "At whatever point you judge the other, you ... do the same things" (**v 1**). How? Remember that the majority of Paul's list of wickedness in 1:29-30 is not about our actions; rather, he is focusing on our attitudes. We are to look at our hearts before looking at our hands.

His teaching lines up with Jesus' **Sermon on the Mount**, where the Lord says: "You have heard that it was said to the people long ago, 'Do not murder, and anyone who murders will be subject to judgment.' But I tell you that anyone who is angry with his brother will be subject to judgment" (Matthew 5:21-22). For most of us, it is not too hard to get to the end of the day and say: *Well, I haven't murdered anyone.* It is rarer for us honestly to be able to say: *I have not been angry with anyone; I have not treated anyone as though they were not worthy of love.*

So Paul's challenge to "you" in Romans **2:1** is: *When you see someone acting in anger—murdering, for instance—what do you do?* It is, of course, right to be someone who "judges all things" (1 Corinthians 2:15) in the sense of following God's verdict on what is right or wrong—if we don't, we become the people of Romans 1:32, who "approve of those who practice" sin. But to "pass judgment" in **2:1** is not simply saying: *That is wrong,* but accompanying it with a particular attitude, basically saying: *You are lost, and I'm glad because now I feel better about myself.* In other words, to "pass judgment" is to believe that others are worthy of God's judgment while you are not.

The Invisible Tape Recorder

It is even very possible that we would pass judgment on someone for an attitude that we ourselves know we share. John Stott points out that we tend to be far quicker and harsher in our criticism of others than of ourselves. We find all kinds of excuses for our sin—we were tired, or provoked, or it was a lesser evil—while being fast to notice and condemn it in others, without ever considering what burdens they may be carrying. John Stott puts it like this:

> "We work ourselves up into a state of self-righteous indignation over the disgraceful behavior of other people, while the very same behavior seems not nearly so serious when it is ours, rather than theirs." (*The Message of Romans,* page 82)

Condemning others while excusing ourselves is what allows us to hang onto both our self-righteousness *and* our sin. We can feel good about ourselves while indulging in what makes us feel good. All the while, Paul says, "you are condemning yourself."

In other words, on the final day of God's judgment, when I stand before him, the counsel for the prosecution will be... me. "God's judgment against those who do such things is based on truth" (**v 2**). God is scrupulously fair in his judgment. And he will use our own standards, the judgments we made with our own mouths, as the standards by which we are judged (as Jesus warned in Matthew 7:1-5).

It is what the twentieth-century theologian Francis Schaeffer called the "invisible tape recorder." It is as though, unseen, there is a recorder (in this decade, it would be an MP3 recorder!) around each of our necks. It records the things we say to others and about others, about how they ought to live. Then, at the last day, God the Judge will take the tape recorder off your neck and say: *I will be completely fair— I will simply play this tape and judge you on the basis of what your own words say are the standards for human behavior.* Paul asks: "Do you think you will escape God's judgment?" (Romans **2:3**). No one in history can realistically answer: *Yes, I think I will.*

Paul's "Elder Son"

Therefore, self-righteous religion is just as much a rejection of God, and a misunderstanding of his character (**2:4**), as the self-centered irreligion of the end of chapter 1. An atheist suppresses the truth about the existence and nature of God, and uses God's gifts to indulge their own desires, without giving glory or thanks to the Giver. It is a presumptuous contempt for his kindness. It is an attitude which scoffs at the idea of God's wrath, not recognizing its present reality, nor realizing that the only reason its full and final arrival is held back is because: "the Lord … is patient with you, not wanting anyone to perish, but everyone to come to repentance" (2 Peter 3:9).

This is exactly what Paul says in Romans **2:4**; *but he is speaking to a religious person.* A self-righteous person will acknowledge the existence of God, but sees no need for him. They are doing well enough themselves. They are their own savior. Ultimately, they deserve glory for themselves. It is the attitude of the person who welcomes God's wrath on others, but thinks they themselves are entirely exempt. They see no need for **repentance**, and have no realization that God is kindly holding back his judgment in order to give *them* an opportunity to turn to him in humility and for mercy. This, too, is a presumptuous contempt for his kindness.

> A self-righteous person will acknowledge the existence of God, but sees no need for him.

So Romans 1 and 2 are setting before us the same two people that Jesus does in his parable about two sons (Luke 15:11-32). There, Jesus gives us a father with two sons. There is a younger brother, who loves sex with prostitutes and squanders the father's money; he's licentious, he's materialistic, he's disobedient to his father. But then there's a second son; he's obedient, and he's compliant with everything the father says. And yet the point of the parable is that they're both lost, both alienated from the father, and they both need salvation. Now here, Paul is saying exactly the same thing. Romans 1 is about younger brothers, and Paul says: *They're lost, they're condemned, worshiping idols of the hand—sin, the kind of sin everyone thinks of as sin.* Now he turns to older brothers in Romans 2 and he says: *You people who are trying so hard to be good, you think God owes you because you're better: you're lost too!*

Paul says: *You're the same.* We can't see it in our English translations, but when in **2:5** he talks about "your stubbornness and your unrepentant heart," Paul is using two Greek words—*sklerotes* and *ametanoetos*—which in the Septuagint, the Greek Old Testament, are always and only used of those guilty of idolatry (eg: Deuteronomy 9:27). Though religious obedience looks godly, in fact it is a form of idolatry. The religious person may have utterly rejected all the current, external idols that society around is worshiping; statues, or casual sex, or career, and so on; but they have idols in their heart. They find their self-worth in their morality; they find their savior in their rule-keeping. They worship their goodness, because their goodness will save them, right? *Wrong,* says Paul: "You are storing up wrath against yourself for the day of God's wrath" (**v 5**).

Religious People Need the Gospel

Paul is showing that religious people need the gospel as much as unreligious people; and that religious people run from the gospel as much as unreligious people. The heart of the gospel is that God's righteousness has been revealed, so that it can be received (1:16-17). When we rely on anything or anyone but Jesus to give us righteousness, we are refusing to accept the gospel. Relying on God's rules is as much self-reliance and God-rejection as ignoring God's rules.

Any moral person who is satisfied with their spiritual state is denying the **doctrine** of righteousness through faith alone. They think they don't need to be given righteousness, because they have their own. They don't know they need the gospel, so they don't get the gospel! They'll stand up proudly on the last day... until God presses "play" on their MP3 recorder.

How do you know if *you* are the "you" Paul is addressing here? Here are three ways to find out:

1. Do you feel that you are a hopeless sinner, whom God would have a perfect right to cast off this minute because of the state of your life and your heart?

2. When you consider how those outside your church live, do you shake your head and judge in your heart; or do you think: *My heart is by nature just like theirs; it just shows itself differently.*

3. Do you, deep down, think there is no MP3 recorder, or that you can stand before your own judgment when the tape is played? Or have you accepted that your own values will condemn you, and that you will need to be given a right standing that you could never achieve yourself?

Questions for reflection

1. Consider carefully your answers to the three questions above, and then speak to God about them.

2. What are the sins you are tempted to excuse in yourself while condemning them in others?

3. How would you use these verses to speak to someone who thinks that because they are good, they are saved?

PART TWO

Saved by Works

When we stand before the Creator God on the last day for his judgment and verdict, what is the general test by which we will be judged? Paul's answer is surprising. It is not: *We'll be judged on whether or not we have received Christ-won and Christ-given righteousness.* Instead, it is that: "God 'will give to each person according to what he has done.'" Judgment is on the basis of **works**.

> What is the test by which we will be judged? Paul's answer is surprising.

Has Paul changed his mind since Romans 1:16-17, where he said right standing with God is given by him, received by us through faith, and never earned? Does Paul teach that we must add works to faith in order to stand in the judgment? Should Martin Luther—who called 1:16-17 his "breakthrough" verses, enabling him to see he was saved by grace, through faith—have continued reading another twenty verses to discover that he had not broken through at all?!

First, let us give Paul some credit for intelligence! Only twenty verses previously he did say that we are saved apart from the law, or anything we can do. We should start from the assumption that Paul is not quietly or accidentally contradicting himself.

Second, in **2:6** Paul is quoting from Psalm 62. God will "give to each person according to what he has done"—so what have people "done" in this psalm? The answer is illuminating. David, the writer, is contrasting two groups of people. There are those who plot against God's chosen king (v 3-4); who lie, and who say one thing with their lips and do the opposite in their hearts (v 4). They are like the people Paul is talking about in Romans 2:1-3.

The other group finds "rest in God alone;" they know their "salvation comes from him" (Psalm 62:1). They are those who say: "My salvation and my honor depend on God; he is my mighty rock, my refuge" (v 7). What they have "done" is to find salvation from God and make him their center. And it is this attitude that "surely [God] will reward" as he gives to "each person according to what he has done" (v 12). So in Romans **2:6**, Paul is asking both the irreligious person and the religious person to consider what they have "done"— or, rather, not done. Neither has repented (**v 5**), seeking refuge from God's deserved wrath in God's undeserved mercy. Both are seeking honor in themselves.

The Evidence, not the Basis

Third, though, Paul *is* saying that works matter—not as the basis for salvation, but as the evidence that someone has the faith that saves. In Psalm 62, what matters fundamentally is a person's relationship to God, as their refuge, their rock, their salvation—and, as verses 9-10 of the psalm suggest, this *will* be seen in how they perceive their life, and what they do in it. Good works show we have saving faith; they do not add to our faith in saving us.

Here is another way to put it: the apples on an apple tree prove life, but they don't provide it. The apples are the evidence that the apple tree is alive, but the roots are what pull in the nourishment to keep it that way. In the same way, faith in Christ alone provides new life (he gives his righteousness, the righteousness of God, to anyone who believes); but a changed life of righteousness is what proves we have real faith.

We mustn't misread Paul as saying that works need to be added to faith in order for us to be able to stand on the day of judgment. But equally, we mustn't allow our understanding of salvation by grace to diminish the challenge here. If the works of our hands are not being changed and informed by the faith we profess to have, it is right to ask whether our faith is heartfelt and real.

How Do We Know?

What are the indicators of whether or not a heart is right with God? **2:7** gives us two tests:

1. "Persistence in doing good" means that doing good—living in a godly way—has become a persistent life pattern.

2. "Seek glory, honor and immortality" refers to qualities that come from life with God, and are found in life with God. The person who is right does not do good deeds for their own sake. He or she does them because he or she wants to become like God in his character. We are wired to enjoy these three things; glory, honor and immortality are good things to seek. The problem is not with the goals, but with our means. We look for them in created things, not the Creator. We need to seek them where they can be found—in God—and be remade in his image. God will "give eternal life" to those who seek it in knowing him.

Verse 8 then gives us two indicators that a person is not right with God:

1. "Self-seeking" is the tell-tale sign. It means to have a spirit of self-will, or self-glorification—of seeking to be our own Lord and/or Savior. This is something that can be pursued either through being irreligious and licentious, or through being moral, religious and upright.

2. "Reject the truth and follow evil" means there is an unwillingness to be instructed and learn from God's truth. There is a lack of teachability, a refusal to submit to truth outside one's own convictions and heart. Irreligious people do this in a very obvious way, but religious people do it, too! If we want to think of ourselves as righteous through our law-keeping, we are willing to listen to God's commands about how to live; but we ignore his word when it tells us that we must keep it perfectly, and that we don't keep it perfectly, and that we need to be given righteousness that we

cannot earn. If we think we can save ourselves, we reject the truth as much as if we think we do not need to be saved at all.

Verses 9-10 then repeat the teaching of **verses 7-8**, with one difference. Twice he says: "first for the Jew, then for the Gentile." That is, "God does not show favoritism" (**v 11**). Judgment is impartial. What matters is not who we are, but what we do: what matters is not our family or cultural background—Jewish, Christian, church-going, completely cut off from the Bible, and so on—but how we decide to relate to God.

All Judged, All Fairly

There is another aspect to God not showing favoritism, which Paul addresses in **verses 12-15**. In a sense, there are two warnings here. First, those who know what God commands, and don't obey him, "will be judged by the law" (**v 12**). It is dangerous to hear God's law! After all, "it is not those who hear the law who are righteous in God's sight, but it those who obey the law who will be declared righteous" (**v 13**).

It is probably best to read this as a hypothetical situation, as John Stott does. In effect, Paul is saying: *Don't think that knowing the law of God is any use; the only path to righteousness through the law is to obey it... and are you really going to claim you always obey all God's law in all ways?*

Next, Paul introduces a category of Gentiles who don't know the law that Jews possess, and yet these Gentiles obey it. Who are these Gentiles? First, they could be Gentiles who obey the law without having heard of Christ, and so are saved outside of faith in Christ. This cannot be correct, since the consistent teaching of the whole New Testament, and the whole thrust of Paul's argument in these chapters, is that "salvation is found in no one else [other than Jesus Christ], for there is no other name under heaven given to men by which we must be saved" (Acts 4:12, see 4:10).

Second, they could be Gentiles who have become Christians and therefore obey the law which has been written on their hearts, even though they don't possess it externally. This may be right, but it would be strange for Paul, speaking here of how every category of humanity deserves judgment, suddenly to talk of those who are saved; and it is difficult to imagine that Gentile Christians would not have been taught the law—the Old Testament—externally in their church, as well as having it written on their hearts internally by the Spirit.

So the third option is best—that Paul is answering the objection: *How can people be judged according to a standard they didn't know? How can judgment be just, if those who don't know God's law "perish apart from the law"* (Romans **2:12**)? And Paul's answer here is that God's law is inborn in people—for sometimes Gentiles "do ... things required by the law ... even though they do not have the law" (**v 14**). All people know the essential principles of right and wrong behavior and their basis in an objective reality, a standard by which we are to be judged.

C.S. Lewis explains:

"Everyone has heard people ... say things like this: 'How'd you like it if anyone did the same to you?' 'Give me a bit of your orange, I gave you a bit of mine' ... [The man who says this] is appealing to some standard of behavior which he expects the other to know about."   (*Mere Christianity*, page 17)

So, when someone who knows nothing of God does what God wants, because they know it is the "right thing" to do, "they show that the requirements of the law are written on their hearts, their consciences also bearing witness" (**v 15**). We all have an in-built sense that there is right and wrong.

> We all have an in-built sense that there is right and wrong.

Of course, our consciences are not as they should be. We "suppress the truth" about God, and about his standards, so that we can worship and live for other things. Further, we do not always follow our consciences. So sometimes we find our thoughts "accusing" as well as "defending" us—everyone does things they know to be wrong. Paul is saying that God is right to judge those who know the law but have not kept it; and Paul is also warning that God will rightfully judge those who don't know the law externally—because they know it internally, yet have not kept it.

No Wrath, No Cross

These verses are packed, and complex! Where has Paul got to?! That judgment "will take place on the day when God will judge" (**v 16**); and that it will be fair, taking account of "men's secrets"—what their hearts are like. On that day, the "you" of verse 1 will no longer be able to hide their idols of the heart underneath religious observance. Conversely, no one who has humbly received the righteousness God has offered will go unnoticed and unsaved.

Why does Paul add "as my gospel declares"? Because God's just judgment is fundamental to his declaration about God's Son. Without judgment, salvation has no meaning. Without the reality of God's present and future wrath, the cross is emptied of its glory. Paul's concern is to show that the ground on which we stand, Gentile and Jew, irreligious and religious, rule-breaking and rule-keeping, is level. All face judgment, and all deserve wrath. It is only from this ground that we are able to look at the cross and see it clearly. We cannot appreciate who Christ is unless we have first acknowledged who we are. As Charles Simeon, the great preacher of the 18th and 19th centuries, put it:

> We cannot appreciate who Christ is unless we have first acknowledged who we are.

"There are but two objects that I have ever desired ... to behold; the one, is my own vileness; and the other is, the glory of God in the face of Jesus Christ: and I have always thought that they should be viewed together."

(Carus, *Memoirs of the life of the Rev. Charles Simeon*, quoted in John Piper, *The Roots of Endurance,* page 108)

Questions for reflection

1. What difference does truly finding rest, hope and honor in God alone make in someone's life, do you think?

2. How do the indicators on pages 47-48 encourage and/or challenge you?

3. How is your conscience defending you today? How is it accusing you?

4. THE RELIGIOUS NEED THE GOSPEL (PART TWO)

Romans 2:17 reminds us who Paul is talking to through this whole chapter—the religious, Bible-believing Jew, who has read the end of chapter 1 and thought: *I am not like these people.*

So the word "if" in **verse 17** is incendiary. Imagine a good Jew reading this verse. *If I am a Jew? How can you possibly say that, Paul? I am a Jew.* We feel the force of the verse simply by inserting "Christian" for "Jew." Paul turns to church members, professing Christians, and says: *Don't just assume you are fine. If you call yourself a Christian…*

Proud to be Jewish

In the rest of chapter 2, Paul describes the person he's speaking to as morally decent (taking the law seriously—**v 17-24**), and religiously active (being **circumcised**—**v 25-29**). These were the two factors the Jews relied on. Some people are religious but not fastidiously moral; some people are scrupulously moral but not religiously active. The Jews were both. And neither made them righteous.

First, Paul lists six things the Jews were proud of when it came to how they lived—their moral goodness:

1. "You call yourself a Jew" (**v 17**)—they were proud of their nationality, pleased to be Jews.

2. "You rely on the law" (**v 17**)—a pride in having and knowing the law God had revealed to their ancestor, Moses, at Mount Sinai (see Exodus 19 – 31).

3. You "brag about your relationship to God" (Romans **2:17**)—God had chosen Israel to be his people (Exodus 19:4-6).

4. "You know his will and approve of what is superior" (Romans **2:18**)—they were able to make correct **ethical** decisions, and they were able to see the wrong choices others were making. Following the detailed rules and regulations in the law of God gave them a sense of being pleasing to God, particularly as they compared themselves to others.

5. "You are instructed by the law" (**v 18**)—they did not only "have" the law, they had mastered it. They could quote it; cross-reference it; go deep into the details of it.

6. "You are convinced that you are a guide for the blind" (**v 19**)—they know that they can see, and that others cannot because they are lost in idolatry, and so they spread the knowledge of the law.

Paul is not saying there is anything wrong with being a Jew; with having and knowing and internalizing God's law; with using his commands to make ethical decisions; or with seeking to share his ways with others. The problem is that "you rely ... you brag" (**v 17**). It is not the Jewishness, or the having of the law (far less the keeping of it) that is wrong; it is their attitude to their nationality and morality. They are relying on it; making what is moral (good things) into a system of salvation. The content of the law is fine, but using the law as the way to eternal life leads only to death. There is not much difference between the words morality and moralism, but there is an eternal world of difference between making a good thing (morality) into your god (moralism).

> Using the law as a way to life leads only to death.

Moralism is extremely common, and always has been. It is the biggest religion in the world today. It is the religion of people who compare themselves with others, who notice that they are "a lot more decent than other people," and conclude: *If there is a God, he'll certainly accept me. I'm a good person.*

How do we know if we have lapsed into "Christian" moralism as the source of our righteousness? Whenever we brag about something we have done—when we rely on our own action, profession or identity—we are living as **functional** moralists.

It is instructive to insert "Christian" for "Jew" and paraphrase **verses 17-20**: *You call yourself a born-again Christian and you are sure you are right with God because you signed a commitment card, or walked down an aisle, or prayed a prayer, and you really cried that night. You remember you had strong feelings for God, so you must have been converted that night. And, hey, since then you have memorized dozens of Scripture verses, and you know the right answer to a large array of questions. And you've led other people to make a commitment to Christ in the Bible study you lead. And you want to get deep into the Bible—that's why you're reading Romans For You!*

Practice What You Preach

Paul has set his readers up with two straight pitches. Now he throws a swerve ball. **Verse 21**: "You, then, who teach others, do you not teach yourself?" The great twentieth-century British preacher D. Martyn Lloyd-Jones shows how this applies to us as professing Christians:

"As you read your Bible day by day, do you apply the truth to yourself? What is your motive when you read the Bible? Is it just to have a knowledge of it so that you can show others how much you know, and argue with them, or are you applying the truth to yourselves? ... As you read ... say to yourself, 'This is me! What is it saying about me?' Allow the Scripture to search you, otherwise it can be very dangerous. There is a sense in which the more you know of [the Bible], the more dangerous it is to you, if you do not apply it to yourself."

(*Romans Chapters 2:1 – 3:20*, pages 147-149)

The further we go in the Christian life, and the more involved we are in our church's life, the more we need to heed these words. Are we preaching to ourselves before we preach to others? Are we practicing ourselves what we call others to practice?

The Idolatry of Religion

Paul lists three ways in which the self-confident moral Jew he is speaking to is not practicing what he teaches. He steals (**v 21**); he commits adultery; he hates idolatry, yet robs temples (**v 22**).

Moralism fails because we are all inconsistent in our behavior. We have the law, but no one keeps it. We break it in two ways. First, there is occasional outright hypocrisy. This can be spectacular (the pastor who is having an affair, or the elder who is committing fraud at work) or everyday (stealing extra time in our lunch break, "forgetting" to include certain items on a tax form).

Second, there are the continual sins of the heart and motives. This is what Paul likely means in his third charge: "you who abhor idols, do you rob temples?" (**v 22**). It is possible that some Jews, though not worshiping idols themselves, would take them from temples and sell them to others. This would be a lot like writing articles for a pornographic magazine that you would not look at yourself or want your children to see. But there is no evidence that self-professing religious, law-keeping Jews actually did this.

So a more likely explanation is that the term "robbing temples" is figurative. Paul is taking a radical approach to the Ten Commandments, just as Jesus did (Matthew 5:21-48). There, Jesus extends the definition of adultery from the purely external (*I didn't sleep with anyone who wasn't my spouse today. That's the seventh commandment kept.*) to include heart motives: "Anyone who looks at a woman lust-fully has already committed adultery with her in his heart" (v 28).

Paul is using the same principle here. True religion is about the heart motives as much as (or more than) about the actions of the body. He is saying: *Idol-worshiping is more than a physical act. You reject bowing to a statue, but you actually worship the same idol that is under the surface of that statue. If you*

> True religion is about heart motives as much as about actions.

let anything become your meaning in life—power, comfort, approval, possessions, pleasure, control—you are violating the command against idolatry just as much as the statue-worshipers you abhor. If you treat religion as your savior, then you are violating the command, too—you have taken a statue from a pagan temple, renamed it "morality," and worshiped it. In other words, it is quite possible to use religiosity to veil our heart-idols of career, sex, reputation, and so on; or to make religiosity itself our idol.

Diagnosing Empty Faith

How can we tell if our "faith" is empty, dead, and under God's judgment? These verses push us to some potentially uncomfortable self-diagnosis. There are two signs Paul gives us here:

1. There is a theoretical-only stance toward the word of God (Romans **2:21**). The moralist or dead orthodox Christian loves the concepts of truth, but is never changed by them. They often see how a sermon or Bible text ought to convict others, but they seldom (if ever) let it convict *them*. A real Christian finds the Bible "living and active" (Hebrews 4:12); when they hear it or read it, they are convicted, comforted, thrilled, disturbed, melted, slammed down, lifted up. Paul prompts us to ask: *Which am I? Do I teach myself?*

2. There is a moral superiority, an in-built bragging. If you are relying on your spiritual achievements, you will have to "look down" on those who have failed in the same areas. You will be at best cold, and at worst condemning, toward those who are struggling. Rather than speaking words of encouragement to the struggler, helping to lift them up, you speak words of gossip about them to others, to show yourself in a comparatively good light. A sign of this condition is that people don't want to share their problems with you, and you are very defensive if others point out your problems to you.

Questions for reflection

1. What are you relying on to bring you acceptance and confidence and purpose in life?

2. How do you practice what you preach? Are there any areas of your life where you are failing to? How will you change?

3. How do you fare in the self-diagnosis tests above?

PART TWO

Why Moralism Causes Blasphemy

The fatal weakness of moralism is that it cannot protect or prevent the heart from sinning; all it can do is seek to hide that sin. Religiosity has no answer to, and no power to remove, selfishness, lust, envy, anger, pride, and anxiety.

The crushing result of Christian moralism is that it dishonors God (**v 23**). When religious people boast about their law-keeping while breaking the law, usually the only person who cannot see what they are doing is them. "God's name is **blasphemed** among the Gentiles because of you" (**v 24**). This is a convicting principle. A life of religious legalism is always distasteful to those outside the faith. A moralist will be smug (they are good people); over-sensitive (their goodness is their righteousness, so must not be undermined); judgmental (they need to find others worse than them in order to be good); and anxious (have they done enough?).

Worse, irreligious people look at and dislike the God who moralists claim to represent. Paul is thus arguing to the Jews: *You were called to be a light to the world, you think of yourselves as bringing light to those who are in darkness, and yet the world finds your religion totally unattractive. Don't you see that therefore you must have misunderstood it?* We need to pose ourselves the same challenge: is our church community, and are we as individuals, attractive?

> Only the gospel produces people who commend God to the world.

Is our humility, love in hard situations, grace under pressure, and so on obvious for others to see? Are we living as an advertisement for God, or as a "Keep clear" sign? Only the gospel produces churches and people who commend God to the world. Moralism cannot.

Dead Orthodoxy

In **verse 25**, Paul introduces circumcision into his argument. This was the great cultural marker of God's covenant with his people. It was the ceremony by which a male Jew was brought into the covenant community. But circumcision had become part of Jewish pride, the basis for a complacent assumption that their cultural identity bestowed righteousness. Their "relationship" with God had become based on pride, not humble joy.

This is still common today, in two ways. First, many people identify with a religion on the basis of their nationality. Because they are British, they are Anglicans; because they are Italian, they are Catholic; because they are Greek, they are Orthodox. They feel their religion is part of their nationality, and they are proud of it. If you tell them they are lost unless there is something more than that, they feel you are insulting their culture and their country.

But additionally, it is quite possible to put your faith in church membership, belonging to the visible people of God, for your salvation. Again, it is revealing to insert other words for "circumcision" and paraphrase Paul's words in **verses 25-29**: *So what if you have been baptized? So what if you are a church member? This only counts for anything if there has been a real change in your life, if your heart has been truly affected. Don't you know that you are not a Christian if you are only one externally, that real Christianity is not about having confidence in external things? No, a Christian is someone who is a Christian inside; what matters is inner baptism, a heart-membership of God's people. And this is a supernatural work, not a human one.*

It is possible to trust in Christianity, rather than Christ. And this can happen in conservative, evangelical churches. Paul is showing us a condition called "dead **orthodoxy**," where the basic doctrines of the Bible are accurately subscribed to, but do not make any internal difference. There is an intellectual grasp of the gospel, but no internal revolution. This form of "Christianity" is outside-out (it never penetrates the heart), rather than true gospel faith, which is inside-out (everything we do flows from who we are internally).

Dead orthodoxy makes the church into a religious cushion for people who think they are Christians, but in fact are radically and subconsciously insecure about their acceptance before God. So every Sunday, people gather to be reassured that they are all right. Various churches offer this reassurance in different ways:

> Dead orthodoxy makes the church into a religious cushion for the insecure.

- Legalistic churches produce detailed codes of conduct and details of doctrine. Members need continually to hear that they are more holy and accurate, and that the "**liberals**" are wrong. They functionally rely on their theological correctness. Sound doctrine equals righteousness.

- Power churches put great emphasis on miracles and spectacular works of God. Members need continually to have powerful or emotional experiences and see dramatic occurrences. They rely on their feelings, and on dramatic answers to prayer. Great emotion equals righteousness.

- Sacerdotal churches put great emphasis on rituals and tradition. Guilt-ridden people are anaesthetized by the beauty of the music and architecture, and the grandeur and mystery of the ceremony. Following **liturgy** equals righteousness.

Of course theological accuracy, moral conscientiousness, praying in faith, being powerfully affected by gospel truths and beautiful worship are all good things! But these elements are so easily, and so regularly, used as a form of "dead works"—replacements for reliance on the righteousness revealed by God in Christ, and received by us in Christ. Richard Lovelace says:

> "Much that we have interpreted as a defect of sanctification [lack of Christian maturity and stability] in church people is really an outgrowth of their loss of bearing with respect to justification [the basis on which we are acceptable to God]."
>
> (*Dynamics of Spiritual Life*, page 211)

The importance of this principle cannot be overemphasized. Again, it prompts us to self-reflection. Along with a theoretical-only approach to God's word, and a sense of (often unconscious) moral superiority, a hallmark of dead orthodoxy is a total lack of an "inner life." But what matters is not bearing the sign (be it circumcision, baptism, church membership card, and so on) but having the reality which the sign signifies. In effect, Paul says in **verses 25-27** that it is better to be an unbaptized believer than a baptized non-believer (and that both are possible). What matters isn't being a "Jew ... outwardly," circumcised physically (**v 28**), but a "circumcision of the heart, by the Spirit" (**v 29**).

This is a vivid image! A circumcised heart is one spiritually melted and softened. It means to have an active prayer life—not out of a sense of obligation or duty, but out of love, because there is a sense of the presence, nearness and goodness of God. (This is not to say that Christians always have great quiet times!) That is something that the moralistic person does not have. They may get "feelings" when they are caught up in the liturgy or excitement or preaching of a corporate service, but they are radically unsure that God loves them, so there is, from Sunday evening through to the next Sunday morning, a sense of deadness, emptiness, and insecurity.

Christians have been Circumcised

None of us want to discover on the last day that we were, in truth, moralists, orthodox in theology and worship but dead spiritually. But the circumcision, the change, the belonging that we need is "of the heart ... not by the written code;" and it is done "by the Spirit," not by men (**v 29**). This is something that cannot be done externally, and that I cannot do myself.

Where is the hope? It is in what circumcision was a sign of. It's worth asking: *Why circumcision?* When God gave **Abraham** an outward sign of the inward reality of his personal, intimate relationship with his Creator, why did he say: "You shall be circumcised" (Genesis 17:9-14)? What is the symbolism of circumcision?

It was a visual sign of the penalty for breaking **covenant**. In ancient times, you didn't sign your name to bind a deal. You acted out the curse that you would accept if you broke covenant. So a man might pick up some sand and drop it on his head to say: *If I break the promises I have made on this day, may I become as this dust.* Or he may cut an animal in half and walk between the pieces to say: *If I disobey this covenant, may I die as this animal has* (this is what God did in sealing his covenant with Abraham, Genesis 15:9-21).

Circumcision (don't think about this too long!) is a cutting off in a very intimate, personal, tender way. So what God was saying to Abraham was: *If you want to be in relationship with me, you need to be circumcised as a sign to you and everyone that, if you break covenant, you will be cut off completely. Cut off from others, cut off from life, cut off from me. You really will be circumcised.*

But no one does keep the covenant (Paul has devoted Romans 2 to making this clear!) So how can God have any people at all? How can anyone be right with him?

Because the "cutting off" of which circumcision was a sign has already happened. Talking about the cross to Colossian Gentile Christians (believers who had not been physically circumcised), Paul says: "In him [Jesus] you were also circumcised … not … by the hands of men but

> In his death, Jesus was cut off. He was truly circumcised.

with the circumcision done by Christ" (Colossians 2:11). He tells them that they have in fact been circumcised, in Christ, on the cross. In his death, Jesus was cut off. He was forsaken by his Father, cut off from him (Mark 15:34). He was "cut off from the land of the living" (Isaiah 53:8). He was truly circumcised. He was bearing the curse of covenant-breaking. He was suffering the curse that law-breakers, whether religious or unreligious, deserve. In him we were circumcised.

When the Spirit works in someone, he gives them the Son's circumcision. Neither our religious performance nor our lack of religious performance matters. Through the Spirit applying the work of the Son to us, the Father sees us as objects of praise, not condemnation (Romans **2:29**). We don't need to praise ourselves, or live for the praise of others. Our Father in heaven sees us as beautiful!

The "written code" leaves us facing the covenant curse, and never deserving of its blessings. We need Another to take our "cut-offness." Only God can do this for us. In the finished work of his Son, and the internal work of his Spirit, he has.

Questions for reflection

1. Have you experienced people rejecting God because of the hypocrisy of those who say they're his people? How can you use your own life to recommend God?

2. Which "dead orthodoxy" do you think you, and your church, would be most likely to fall into? How can you prevent this?

3. Meditate on the circumcision Christ underwent on your behalf. How does this move you to praise him and love him?

5. EVERYONE NEEDS THE GOSPEL

Paul has been cutting away any grounds we may think we have for being right in God's sight. It makes uncomfortable reading, both for the unreligious person and, perhaps more so, for the **professing** Christian. In this section, Paul moves relentlessly toward his conclusion: that "no-one will be declared righteous in [God's] sight by observing the law" (**Romans 3:20**).

Meeting People Where They're At

In the first eight verses of the chapter, Paul anticipates and answers some objections he knows chapter 2 may have provoked among those in the Roman church who are from a Jewish background. These objections are not critical to Paul's argument, and they may not be objections we often hear raised today. But Paul was a great **evangelist**, and we see him here placing himself in his listeners' shoes, respecting them enough to think hard about how they would be responding to his teaching (he does something similar in Acts 17:22-31 as he preaches in Athens). We learn much from the very fact that Romans **3:1-8** is here.

These verses are thus best understood as a Q+A session between Paul and his imagined reader:

Q: Paul, are you saying there is no advantage to biblical religion (**v 1**)?

A: No, I'm not saying that. There is great value in having and knowing the words of God (**v 2**).

Q: Yes, but those words have failed, haven't they, because so many haven't believed the gospel of righteousness revealed in God's Son Jesus. What has happened to the promises (**v 3a**)?

A: Despite his people's failure to believe, God's promises to save are advancing. Our faithlessness only reveals how committed to his truth he is (think of what he's done in order to be faithful to his promises!) (**v 3b-4**).

Q: But if unrighteousness is necessary for God's righteousness to be seen, how is it fair for him to judge us (**v 5**)?

A: On that basis, God would not judge anyone in the world. And we (ie: Paul and religious Jews) all agree God should judge (**v 6**).

Q: Well then, if me sinning makes God look better, that means that I should sin more, shouldn't I, so that his glory is more clearly seen (**v 7-8**)?

A: I've been accused of thinking this, and I certainly don't. And saying you're sinning so that God will love you is an attitude that is absolutely worthy of judgment (**v 8**).

All Lost

"What shall we conclude then?" (**v 9**). Here is where Paul has been leading us since 1:18. And the conclusion is: everyone is "under sin." "There is no one righteous" (**3:10**). To be "under sin" and to be "unrighteous" are the same thing. To be unrighteous is a positional term; we stand before God not in right standing with him, or others, because we have wronged him and them. To be "under sin" is a legal term; we are citizens of sin. It is as though we all have a spiritual passport, which shows our legal citizenship. It is either stamped *Under sin* or *Under grace*. And Paul's astounding statement is that Jews and Gentiles, religious and unreligious, are *all* under sin. The person who lives a life of tremendous immorality and debauchery, who fits every description of 1:18-32, and the person who is conscientious and moral are *alike* under sin.

This does not mean that every person is as sinful as every other person. It means that our legal condition is the same. We are all lost, and there are no degrees of lostness.

Imagine three people try to swim from Hawaii to Japan. One cannot swim at all; he sinks as soon as he gets out of his depth. The next is a weak swimmer; he flounders for sixty feet before drowning. The third is a championship swimmer and swims

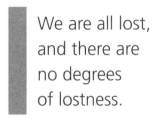

We are all lost, and there are no degrees of lostness.

strongly for a long time. But after thirty miles he is struggling; after forty he is sinking; after fifty miles he drowns. Is one more drowned than the others? No! It doesn't matter at all which swam further; none were anywhere near Japan, and each ends as dead as the others. In the same way, the religious person may trust in morality and the pagan indulge in sensuality, and neither comes close to a righteous heart. They are equally lost, equally condemned to perish. We "alike are all under sin" (**3:9**).

How Sin Affects Sinners

Next, Paul gives a long list of sin's effects on us. Not only do we need to accept that we are sinners; we need also to begin to grasp the problem of the reality of our sinfulness. As Paul provides layer after layer of evidence, we see in stark terms who we are, and what this means for us. There are seven effects that sin has:

1. Our legal standing. No one is legally righteous, and no one's deeds can change that. We are guilty and condemned (**v 10**).

2. Our minds. "There is no one who understands" (**v 11**). Because our core nature is corrupted by sin, we don't understand God's truth. We are "darkened in [our] understanding ... because of the ignorance that is in [us] due to the hardening of [our] hearts" (Ephesians 4:18). Ignorance does not cause hardness of hearts (we don't know about God, so we don't love him); instead, heart-hardness causes lack of understanding. That is because our sinful self-centeredness leads us to filter out a lot of reality. It is a form of denial; we are blind to many truths and our thinking does not compute data as it should.

3. Our motives. "No one seeks God" (Romans **3:11b**). None of us really want to find him; rather, we are running and hiding from him in all we do, even in our religion and morality (we'll think more about this below).

4. Our wills. "All have turned away" (**v 12**). This carries echoes of Isaiah 53:6: "All we like sheep have gone astray; we have turned every one to his own way" (KJV). There is a willfulness about our wandering. Sin can be defined as our demand for self-determination, for the right to choose our own paths.

5. Our tongues. "Their throats are open graves" (Romans **3:13**). We are deceitful, poisonous, bitter and cursing in what we say (**v 13-14**). The image is that of a grave with rotting bodies in it. Sinful words are signs of decay. We use our tongues to lie to protect our own interests, and to damage the interests of others.

6. Our relationships. We are "swift to shed blood; ruin and misery mark [our] ways, and the way of peace [we] do not know" (**v 15-17**). This is how sin affects our relationships: we are after each other's blood—sometimes literally, more often in seeking to push down those who get in our way. Why do we become angry with people? Because they have blocked us from access to an idol—they have compromised our comfort, or prevented a promotion, or made us feel out of control, or are enjoying a relationship we feel we need. When we do not live enjoying God's approval in the gospel, we do not know peace ourselves, nor can we live in peace with others.

7. Our relationship to God. "There is no fear of God before [our] eyes" (**v 18**).

This is a detailed, depressing list. It also contains two particularly surprising claims, and a striking conclusion. Paul claims that "no one ... seeks God" and that "no one ... does good." "No fear of God" is both a summary of, and the pointer to the antidote for, our sin.

Why Seekers Aren't Seeking God

Seeking after God (**3:11**) should be understood in its obvious meaning. It is a desire to know the true God, to find and enjoy *him*; a desire to worship, appreciate and rejoice in him for who he is.

Many will say: *Paul has gone too far here. I know many people who aren't Christians and who don't go to church—but they pray, and they think hard; they are searching profoundly for the truth. And then there are people in other religions, too. And after all, I was once a seeker, and I found God!*

But Paul isn't saying: *No one seeks for spiritual blessings* or *No one seeks God to answer their prayers* or *No one is seeking to have spiritual power or peace or experiences.* He does not say these things because many, many people do them. What Paul is saying is: *No one, prompted by their own decision and acting in their own ability, wants to find God.*

Here's what he means. Someone might have an intellectual interest in the possibility of God, or a philosophical conviction that there is a God. But that is not a real passion to meet with God. In fact, both can be a way of avoiding meeting the real God—if we can keep him in the realm of intellectual argument or philosophical construct, we can keep ourselves from having to deal with the objective reality of the true God.

Or, someone might have a problem in their lives and realize that they need forgiveness to deal with their guilt; or spiritual peace to deal with their anxiety; or power or wisdom to be able to and know how to move forward in life; or a **mystical** experience to deal with the emptiness they feel. But that is not the same thing at all as truly seeking to know, and be known by, the holy, living, sovereign, relational God. It is seeking what God can give us, but not seeking him.

Paul is saying that sinful self-centeredness controls all spiritual searching for meaning and experience, so that we will try simply to get blessings from God, keeping control ourselves and expecting (or demanding) that God serve us and shape himself to fit our needs. We won't bow down before the living God, giving him control of our lives and futures, enjoying him for who he is and experiencing his blessings in relationship with him as we ask him to shape us as we serve him.

> Anyone who is truly seeking God has been sought by God.

This means that anyone who is truly seeking God has been sought by God. If no one is capable of seeking God, then any human who is truly searching for him must have already undergone some change inside them that is caused by God's Spirit, not their own. Jesus himself said: "No one can come to me unless the Father who sent me draws him" (John 6:44, see also v 65). Paul hopes for the ungodly that "God may perhaps grant them repentance leading to a knowledge of the truth" (2 Timothy 2:25, ESV). Turning to God as Lord, and knowing the truth about who he is and who we are, are not things we do so that God will work in us; they are works God does in us so that we can find him.

When we consider our own path to finding God, we need to realize that we did not seek him out; he drew us to him. We decided to put our faith in him only because he had decided to give us faith. What difference does this make? You rejoice to see that God is not trying to hide from you, that all the things you know about him he has chosen to reveal to you. You are humbled by the truth that there is nothing better or cleverer in you which means you sought God; that you have nothing that you weren't given (1 Corinthians 4:7). You are comforted and confident "that he who began a good work in you will carry it on to completion until the day of Christ Jesus" (Philippians 1:6). And you praise God with greater gratitude, because you know that everything about your salvation comes from him, from first to last. Salvation did not begin with you deciding to seek God, but with him choosing to seek you. You know that everything you have and are is by sheer grace. You sing:

'Tis not that I did choose thee, for Lord, that could not be;
This heart would still refuse thee, hadst thou not chosen me ...
My heart owns none before thee, for thy rich grace I thirst;
This knowing, if I love thee, thou must have loved me first.

Questions for reflection

1. How do you feel about Paul's claim that "all [are] under sin"? Why do you feel like that?

2. How do you see the effects of your sin on your life, thoughts and relationships?

3. How do you respond to the truth that God sought you out before you sought him out? What difference will it make to you?

PART TWO

Why Goodness Isn't Always Good

If it seemed an exaggeration for Paul to say that no one seeks God, it will certainly appear outrageous for him to claim that "no one does good" (Romans **3:12**).

Now, how can Paul say this? After all, many non-Christians do many good things, using their talents and wealth in ways which are kind and generous and which make the world a better place. And the Lord Jesus himself commanded us to do "good works" (Matthew 5:16).

But we need to remember what kind of "goodness" Paul is talking about here. His focus is on our relationship to God, and whether our good deeds can fix that broken relationship; whether they can establish a righteousness of our own. The teaching is that, ultimately, our good deeds cannot do anything to get us saved. In fact, they can leave us further from, not closer to, righteousness.

The Bible sees a truly good deed as being good in form *and* in motive. For example, if you help an old lady across the street, that is good in form; it conforms to God's will for our behavior. But *why* are you helping her? If it is because it is dark on the other side and you will be able to rob her; or (less extreme, and more likely) it is because you are hoping she will give you some money in gratitude; or because you have seen a friend further down the street who you know will notice and be impressed—then your good work arises from a selfish heart and selfish motives. But a good deed in God's sight is one done for his glory, not our own (1 Corinthians 10:31).

The nineteenth-century preacher C.H. Spurgeon reputedly often told a story which gets to the heart of this:

Once in a kingdom long ago, a gardener grew a huge carrot. He decided to give it to his prince because he loved his sovereign. When he gave it, the prince discerned his love and devotion, and the fact that he expected nothing in return. So as the gardener turned to leave, he said: "Here, my son, I want to give you some of my land so that you can produce an even greater crop. It is yours." The gardener went home rejoicing. A nobleman heard of this incident and thought: "If that is what the prince gives in response to the gift of a carrot, what would he give me if I gave him a fine horse?" So the nobleman came and presented the prince with a fine steed as a gift. But the prince discerned his heart and said: "You expect me to give to you as I did to the gardener. I will not. You are very different. The gardener gave me the carrot. But you were giving yourself the horse."

If you know God loves you in Christ, and that there is nothing you can do or need to do but accept his perfect righteousness, then you can feed the hungry, visit the sick, and clothe the naked, and all of it will be done as a gift to God. But if you think you are going to get or keep your salvation by doing these good deeds, it is really yourself you are feeding, yourself you are clothing, yourself you are visiting. It is who we are serving in our hearts that matters, not how we are serving with our hands. Without faith in Christ, good deeds are not truly done for God, but for ourselves—and thus are not truly good.

This is why any goodness we have becomes sour. If we do good to gain God's favor, blessing and salvation, and do well, we will be smug, superior, and complacent; if we do badly, we will be anxious, self-pitying, and angry. The "good deeds" done outside trusting the gospel will make a soul go sour.

> The main difference between a Christian and a religious person is their attitude toward their "good deeds."

All of us have to understand this to be saved Christians, rather than unsaved-but-religious people. The main difference between a Christian and a religious person is not so much their attitudes to their sins, but toward their "good deeds." Both will repent of their sins; but only the Christian will repent of wrongly-motivated good works, while the religious person will rely on them. The eighteenth-century preacher George Whitefield said:

"Our best duties are as so many splendid sins ... you must not only be made sick of your ... sin, but you must be sick of your righteousness, of all your duties and performances. There must be a deep conviction before you can be brought out of your self-righteousness; it is the last idol taken out of your heart."

(*Sermon 58*, from J.C. Ryle,
The Select Sermons of George Whitefield)

No Fear

Verse 18 is Paul's summary of everything he has said from Romans **3:10** onward. Where do the ignorance of God (**v 11**), willful independence from God (**v 12**), and selfish good deeds (**v 12**), words (**v 13-14**) and actions (**v 15-17**) come from? "There is no fear of God before their eyes" (**v 18**).

The "fear of God" is a central concept in the Bible. We are repeatedly told: "The fear of the Lᴏʀᴅ is the beginning of wisdom" (eg: Psalm 111:10). It is the starting point for everything else; it is the stumbling block which bars everything else. What is the "fear of God"? The psalmist says something surprising: "If you, O Lᴏʀᴅ, kept a record of sins, O Lᴏʀᴅ, who could stand? But with you there is forgiveness; therefore you are feared" (Psalm 130:3-4). He "fears" God because God forgives sins! So the "fear of God" does not mean a servile, cringing fear of punishment. It means, rather, an inner attitude of awe, respect, and sober, trembling joy before the greatness of God. Another way to put this is in Psalm 16:8: "I have set the Lᴏʀᴅ always before me." He is saying: *My secret is that I live my life keeping the greatness of God always before me. I always think of his glory, love, and power; and I let who he is control me at all times. I live in light of him.*

And so "fearing God" is the antidote to everything Paul says about sin. Take two of the effects of sin that Paul lists:

■ "No one … seeks God" (Romans **3:11**). Sin is characterized by running from God. Sin makes you forget God, makes him unreal to you. It is the opposite of fearing God, in which your passion is to come before him and always think of him. So there are the two ways to live life: forgetting his reality, and being aware of his reality.

■ "Their throats are open graves" (**v 13**). It is only if the glory and love of God are unreal to you that you can lie or harm with the tongue, or that you can fight with people or be willful in the heart.

The Spiritual Condition of Silence

All the way through this section—even in 1:18-32, when he was talking about sinful pagans who deserve and experience God's wrath—Paul has been speaking primarily to the "religious." That is, he is talking to law-keeping, Bible-believing, self-righteous people. This is why Paul has quoted the Old Testament Scriptures in his description of the effects of sin in **3:10-18**. This is what the "law" says people are like—and Paul has shown that the people whom it is describing are Jews as well as Gentiles. "Whatever the law says, it says to those who are under the law" (**v 19**). It applies to everyone who knows and seeks to keep the law, just as much as to those who don't know or don't care about it.

So the effect of knowing the law should not be a proud claim that I am a good law-keeper, that I stand right with God. Its effect should be that: "every mouth may be silenced and the whole world held accountable to God" (**v 19**). The law is not given to us so that, in observing it, we can "be declared righteous" (**v 20**), because we are all sinful. The law is not a checklist we keep; it is a benchmark we fail. "Through the law we become conscious of sin." Whenever someone reads God's law, however loyal, kind, thoughtful, generous or loving they are, their response can only be: *I am a sinner. I have nothing to* *say to God—no defense to make or offer to make. I am in desperate trouble.*

This is a bleak truth; but hard truth is better than sweet deceit. And it makes sense of what we see in and around us. The seventeenth-century mathematician and philosopher Blaise Pascal put it like this:

"Nothing offends us more rudely than this doctrine, yet without this mystery, the most incomprehensible of all, we are incomprehensible to ourselves." (*Pensées*, Section VII, 434)

A silent mouth is thus a spiritual condition. It is the condition of the person who knows that they cannot save themselves. As John Gerstner explains:

> A silent mouth is a spiritual condition.

"The way to God is wide open. There is nothing standing between the sinner and his God. He has immediate and unimpeded access to the Savior. There is nothing to hinder. No sin can hold [you] back, because God offers justification to the ungodly. Nothing now stands between the sinner and God but the sinner's 'good works.' Nothing can keep him from Christ but his delusion ... that he has good works of his own that can satisfy God ... All they need is need. All they must have is nothing ... But alas, sinners cannot part with their 'virtues.' They have none that are not imaginary, but they are real to them. So grace becomes unreal. The real grace of God they spurn in order to hold on to the illusory virtues of their own. Their eyes fixed on a mirage, they will not drink real water. They die of thirst with water all about them."

(*Theology for Everyman*, page 72-73)

"In the gospel, a righteousness from God is revealed" (1:16). All we need do is come to Christ with empty hands and receive his righteousness. What keeps people from salvation is not so much their sins, but their good works. If we come to God telling him that we are good, offering him the works of our hands as our righteousness, we cannot take the righteousness he gives by grace. We need to give up our goodness, and repent of our religiosity as well as our rebellion. We need to come with empty hands, and silent mouths, and receive.

Questions for reflection

1. Why do rebels need the gospel? How would you explain this to someone who rejects the existence of God?

2. Why do good people need the gospel? How would you explain this to someone who thinks they are good enough for God?

3. Why do you need the gospel? How do you remind your heart of this when it is tempted to feel pride about goodness or despair about sin?

6. A DIAMOND ON A BLACK CLOTH

"But" is a word that reverses the statement which has gone before; it can qualify praise, or bring hope where there seemed to be none. This is why there are few words more glorious than the "but" that begins Romans **3:21**. "No one will be declared righteous … through the law we become conscious of sin" (v 20)… *But…* Paul now turns from the black cloth of human sin to hold up the glittering diamond of the gospel.

Righteousness and Justification

The gospel, as we know from 1:17, reveals a "righteousness from God" (**3:21**); or "the righteousness *of* God" (ESV). It is a righteousness *displayed*; but it is also a righteousness *granted*. Our translations sometimes obscure this, but the words "righteousness" and "justified" in these verses are all the same word: *dikaiosune*. So, **verse 21** could read: *But now a justification from/of God has been made known*; **verse 24** could be translated: *and are righteousnessed freely.*

Righteousness is a validating performance record which opens doors. When you want a job, you send in a resumé. It has all the experiences and skills that make you (you hope!) worthy of the position. You send it in and say: *Look at this. Accept me!* Your record has nothing on it that disqualifies you from the job; and it has (you hope!) everything that will qualify you for it.

Every religion and culture believes that it's the same with God. It's not a vocational record; it's a moral or spiritual record. You get out your performance record and if it's good enough, you're worthy of life with God and you're accepted. And then Paul comes along and says: *But now…* For the first time in history—and the last—an unheard of approach to God has been revealed. A divine righteousness—the righteousness of *God*, a perfect record—is *given* to us.

No other place offers this. Outside of the gospel, we must develop a righteousness, and offer it to God, and say (hopefully and anxiously): *Accept me.* The gospel says that God has developed a perfect righteousness, and he offers it to us, and by it we are accepted. This is the uniqueness of the Christian gospel; and it reverses what every other religion and **worldview**, and even every human heart, believes.

How Righteousness Comes

Verses 22-25 teach us four lessons about how righteousness comes to sinful people.

First, it "comes through faith in Jesus Christ to all who believe" (**v 22**). Righteousness-receiving faith has one object: Christ. President Eisenhower is reputed to have once said that America was "founded on a deeply-felt religious faith—and I don't care what it is." This is a typical view today; any other is seen as dogmatic and undemocratic. But it is the object of belief, rather than the belief itself, which is the crucial issue. I may have great, unshakeable faith in the ability of feathers strapped to my arms to fly me from the US to the UK; but I have put my faith in the wrong place. Equally, I may have just barely enough faith to board a transatlantic flight, trembling nervously as I do; and yet the object of my faith will accomplish what it promises. It is not faith that saves; it is not even faith in God that saves: it is faith *in Jesus Christ.*

Second, it cannot come through our own actions or efforts (**v 23**). Literally, verse 23 says: "All have sinned and lack the glory of God." We were made in God's image to bring him glory and enjoy the glory of his praise (2:29). In our sin, we have lost this glory; we cannot live in the presence of God, enjoying his approval.

Third, it is given "freely" (**3:24**). This is very important, because it is possible to think of faith as a kind of "work," a calling up of some psychological feeling about God. Some people think of faith as an intense attitude of surrender or a state of certainty or confidence. But Paul takes care to say it comes "freely." This is the word used when Jesus Christ says: "They hated me *without a cause*" (John 15:25, ESV). The word "freely" means without a cause, in a way that is totally and wholly unwarranted, given or done for no reason. We must not fall prey to the subtle mistake of thinking that our faith actually saves us, as though in the Old Testament God wanted obedience to the law for salvation, and now he has changed the requirements and all he wants is faith. That is a misunderstanding of both the Testaments, of the role of both law and faith! In both the Old and New Testaments, it is the work of Christ that merits our salvation. In both, faith is how it is received, and that is all it is. Faith is simply the attitude of coming to God with empty hands. When a child asks his mother for something he needs, trusting that she will give it, his asking does not merit anything. It is merely the way he receives his mother's generosity.

> Faith is simply the attitude of coming to God with empty hands.

This is crucial because, if you come to think that your belief is the cause of your salvation, you will stop looking at Christ and start looking at your faith. When you see doubts, it will rattle you. When you don't feel it quite as clearly or excitedly, it will worry you. What has happened? You've turned your faith into a "work"! Faith is only the instrument by which you receive your salvation, not the cause of your salvation. If you don't see this, you will think you have something to boast about: *The reason I am saved is because I put my faith in Jesus*. This is a subtle misunderstanding which cuts away our assurance, and boosts our pride. And verse 27 says the gospel leaves no basis for boasting.

Fourth and last, Paul is even more specific about what we must have faith *in*. It is faith in Christ's work on the cross, rather than a general admiration of him as a great man, or as an inspirational example, and so on. Righteousness comes "through faith in his blood" (Romans **3:25**). Saving faith is in "Jesus Christ *and him crucified*" (1 Corinthians 2:2).

And so "all who believe" (Romans **3:22**) are made righteous. "There is no difference" because, since we are all sinners, there is no one who does not need to receive righteousness; and because, since Christ died for those sins, there is no one who cannot receive righteousness.

Martyn Lloyd-Jones sums it up:

"The man who has faith is the man who is no longer looking at himself, and no longer looking to himself. He no longer looks at anything he once was. He does not look at what he is now. He does not look at what he hopes to be … He looks entirely to the Lord Jesus Christ and his finished work, and he rests on that alone."   (*Romans Chapters 3:20 – 4:25*, page 45)

How Righteousness *Can* Come

But how can God remain righteous—maintain a perfect record of being just and always doing what is right—*and* make sinners, who deserve justice, righteous? How can there be a righteousness *of* God and a righteousness *from* God? How can a just God justify justifying you and me?

"Through the redemption that came by Christ Jesus" (**v 24**). Redemption is a word that takes us back to Old Testament Israel. In that agricultural society, it did not take much to get into debt, into having to sell yourself into slavery, but it did take much—your whole life, perhaps—to get out of it. So God's law made provision for a kinsman-redeemer—a *go'el*—who would buy you out of that debt, that slavery, so you could live free again (Leviticus 25:25). Now Paul says that through Jesus, to us who are slaves to sin and death and judgment… to us who can never pay the debt that we owe… to us redemption—freedom from that debt—has come.

The Father justifies his people through the work of his Son. He redeemed us by: "present[ing] him [Jesus] as a sacrifice of atonement" (**v 25**). Here is the way that the just God justifies sinners; how he makes the unrighteous righteous.

Much has been written about how to translate the word Paul uses here, *hilastrion*. The NIV uses the term "sacrifice of atonement;" the KJV and ESV render it "propitiation." Several other modern translations (eg: RSV, NEB) put in the word "expiation," but that is because the translators want to avoid the clear meaning of the word Paul uses. Expiation is the wiping away of wrongdoing. Propitiation includes expiation, but is much more than expiation—it is the turning away of God's wrath. It means that God's wrath is turned away from us—those who deserve it—by the provision of One who takes it in our place: God himself, Jesus.

So the cross is the place where the Judge takes the judgment. This was the Father's plan, and it was also the Son's willing sacrifice. He did not suffer because he had to, but because he loved His Father and us. He could have turned aside, but chose not to (Mark 14:35-36).

If God forgave us by becoming indifferent to sin—if the only way he could justify his people was to give up his role as Judge—then that would hardly be loving to the victims of sin, it would give us no assurance for the future, and would make God deeply compromised within his character. No, God should, must, and will judge us. The wonder is that he judged us in the person of his own Son; that, as John Murray writes:

"God loved the objects of his wrath so much that he gave his own Son to the end that he by his blood should make provision for the removal of his wrath."
(*The Atonement*, page 15)

God does not set his justice aside; he turns it onto himself. The cross does not represent a compromise between God's wrath and his love; it does not satisfy each halfway. Rather, it satisfies each fully and in the very same action.

> God does not set his justice aside; he turns it onto himself.

On the cross, the wrath and love of God were both vindicated, both demonstrated, and both expressed perfectly. They both shine out, and are utterly fulfilled. The cross is a demonstration both of God's justice, and of his justifying love (Romans **3:25-26**).

Sins Committed Beforehand

Understanding the cross enables us to understand Paul's words in **verse 25**: that God "left the sins committed beforehand unpunished."

If God had really and totally forgiven the sins committed by his Old Testament people, they would be gone; nothing more would need to be done. But Paul is showing us that in fact God had not forgiven them, so much as left them unpunished, until he punished his Son for them at the cross. In other words, God in his patience had deferred payment on those sins. The sacrifices and rituals of the Old Testament were only and always place-holders pointing to Christ; they did not really pay the debts (as the New Testament books of Galatians and Hebrews explain in far more detail). God was accepting Abraham, Moses, David and all the Old Testament saints when they repented and trusted in his mercy, but he accepted them on the basis of the future work of Christ. He was already the just Judge who justifies his people.

Losing Justice or Justification

What happens if we forget that God is "just," or forget that he is "the one who justifies"? Unless your God is a God of both sacrificial love and holy anger against evil, it will introduce distortions into your life.

On the one hand, if you object to the idea of a God with standards, and who upholds those standards, you are like a child who strains against the parental limits and who, if he succeeds in leaving them behind, spends his life feeling liberated and yet disoriented, with nothing to rely on, nothing under or around him. We (rightly) hear a lot about abusive, overbearing parents who do not show love to their children. But completely permissive parents who set no limits, give no guidance, and never confront their children are also unloving, and also destructive. The world is full of people raised with a supposedly enlightened view of a "loving," "anything-goes" God, so they feel spiritually like orphans with no certainty or real love, *because they are*. They have ended up with a God who is uncaring and indifferent; and, of course, non-existent.

On the other hand, a wrathful God without grace will never give you the motivation to live a decent life. You will feel crushed and despairing, or angry and defiant, and always be unloving, because fear can't produce love. If you have a God only made of standards and judgment, you will be a driven person, never able to live up to his standards, always fleeing from him.

The wonder of the cross is that in the very same stroke it satisfies both the love of God and the justice of God. At the very same moment it shows us that God is *both* the Judge, who cares enough about his world to set standards and hold us accountable to them; *and* the Justifier, who has done everything necessary to forgive and restore us. He is a Father worth having, and he is a Father we can have. The cross is where,

> God is a Father worth having, and a Father we can have.

gloriously and liberatingly, we see that he is "just and the one who justifies those who have faith in Jesus" (**Romans 3:26**).

Questions for reflection

1. If you had a minute in an elevator to explain to someone how we can be right with God, what would you say?

2. Do you tend to forget God's justice, or God's justification? How does forgetting one or the other affect your feelings, your outlook, and/or your actions?

3. How has this section moved you to praise the God who justifies?

PART TWO

The Boasting Issue

Paul has presented us with a dazzling explanation of the gospel. What lesson does he draw? "Boasting ... is excluded" (**v 27**).

The word "boasting" comes from the battlefield. As a soldier, how could you get the confidence to advance out into battle against the enemy? By saying (in your heart, and in shouting to them): *We're bigger and stronger than you. We have more men or better weapons than you. We're going to beat you.* It's what we see Goliath doing before the Israelite ranks in 1 Samuel 17:8-11.

What you boast in is what gives you confidence to go out and face the day. It is the thing of which you say: *I am a somebody because I have that. I can beat what comes against me today because I am this.* What you boast in is what fundamentally defines you; it is where you draw your identity and self-worth from.

Now, in the gospel boasting is "excluded." Why? A great way to understand what Paul means is to look

> You boast in what gives you confidence to go out and face the day.

at his own experience. In Philippians 3:5-11, Paul tells us what, before he became a Christian, he had confidence in; what he boasted in: "Circumcised on the eighth day, of the people of Israel, of the tribe of Benjamin, a **Hebrew** of Hebrews; in regard to the law, a **Pharisee**; as for **zeal**, persecuting the church; as for legalistic righteousness, faultless." That is quite some list! It includes family pedigree, racial background, professional and educational attainments and religiosity/ morality.

Then he says: "I consider them rubbish" (v 8)! He has no confidence in them; he doesn't boast about them—quite the opposite. He says: *I don't need any of these things. None of these things help me at all!* What has he given them up for? "That I may gain Christ." Paul is saying that boasting and believing are opposites; you can't do both. The principle of faith excludes boasting (Romans **3:27**) because faith understands that there is nothing we do that justifies us (**v 28**). If we are to receive Jesus, we must give up boasting.

> Boasting and believing are opposites; you can't do both.

This is more challenging and offensive than it may at first appear. Paul is saying that we must give up all our sense of identity and security; all our grounds of dignity and self-worth are "excluded." Why? Because "a man is justified by faith apart from observing the law" (**v 28**). After all, God is the God who has made his righteousness available to Jews and to Gentiles (**v 29**). He is the justifying God, to whom both the circumcised (religious people) and the uncircumcised (unreligious people) need to turn in faith (**v 30**).

We only exclude boasting when we realize that our *best* achievements have done nothing to justify us! To boast in them is like a drowning man clutching a fistful of hundred-dollar bills and shouting: *I'm OK! I've got money!*

If you understand the gospel of righteousness received, you will never boast. Or rather, you will never boast in yourself, but you will boast only in someone who is not you, and exclusively about something you did not do: Christ, and him crucified. Paul says he will "never boast except in the cross of our Lord Jesus Christ" (Galatians 6:14). Christians know they are saved solely and wholly by Christ's work, not their own. They take no credit for their standing with God, nor for their blessings from God.

Their boasting is transferred from themselves to their Savior, because everyone will always "boast" in—draw confidence and hope from—the object of their faith. If you know you are saved by Christ's work alone, you have great confidence, but it is not self-confidence in your own works; rather, it is Christ-confidence in his death. You face the day, even the day of your death, saying to the world: *I have Christ. His death means that when God looks at me, he sees his beautiful child. World, I need nothing from you, and you can take nothing from me. I have Christ.*

What Boasting Causes

This boasting-transfer, from works to Christ, changes us completely. Indeed, we can view most of the problems in societies and individuals as the result of misplaced boasting. Here are three:

1. Human divisions. Pride in race, social status, or achievement necessarily leads to prejudice, condescension, and hostility. To get our confidence, we must see ourselves as better than other classes of people.

2. Denial. If our confidence comes from our race/ethnicity, we will have to blind ourselves to the evils and flaws of our people. This leads to racism, classism, etc. If our confidence comes from our moral attainments, we will have to blind ourselves to our sins and selfishness. It makes us tremendously touchy when someone criticizes our religion or moral character, because our moral purity is our only strength. If we lose it, we lose everything. If our confidence comes from someone's love (a parent's, a child's, a spouse's, a romantic partner's), we will have to blind ourselves to the loved one's sins or any problems in the relationship. We will not be able to give "tough love" when needed.

3. Anxiety. When anything we boast in is threatened, our fundamental security is threatened. We are vulnerable to great terror.

The gospel creates a whole new mindset. Its marks include:

1. Your mind is deeply satisfied with the doctrine of justification. You say: *I see it. It's staggering! He accepts me because Jesus paid for all my flaws!* What a wonder! You *never* get tired of thinking about it. You can't get enough of it. It is not a dry doctrine which you simply understand mechanically. It is the well-spring of your

joy, a truth that makes your heart sing—because it is about you, and your justification, and your freedom and confidence.

2. A new freedom from denial. The gospel gives you a grounding so that criticism, bad news, and negative evaluations can now be handled. Bad news and abject failure no longer threaten your confidence. Now, the more you see your faults and failures, the more amazing and precious God's love appears, and the more loved by him you feel. This is a critical test! If fundamentally you reject the whole idea of the cross and Jesus as your sin-bearing substitute—if deep down you really think your worthiness and acceptability hang on your performance—then, when your sin is revealed, it drives you away from God instead of it making you feel closer to him.

3. A new freedom from anxiety. Slowly you become a more coura-geous person, not afraid of death or the future or other people. You come to know that God is *for* you. You know that: "He who did not spare his own Son, but gave him up for us all—how will he not also, along with him, graciously give us all things?" (Romans 8:32). So you place your worst fears into his hands and leave them there; you face difficulty and danger by saying: *He is for me so I can face death. I know the future is in his hands. He wouldn't go to all this trouble and not give me what I really need.* When death comes, you take the Lord Jesus' dying words joyfully onto your own lips: "Father, into your hands I commit my spirit" (Luke 23:46).

Is the Law now Nothing?

The law cannot save us. The law gives us no grounds for boasting, for self-worth or for confidence. The righteousness of God, and from God, has been revealed "apart from law" (Romans 3:21). So when Paul poses the question: "Do we, then, nullify the law by this faith?" (**verse 31**), it certainly seems that the answer is: *Yes. All that matters now is receiving by faith the righteousness offered at the cross.*

And yet Paul answers: "Not at all!" and adds that far from making the law null and void, "rather, we uphold the law." He is saying that a gospel believer, who is saved apart from law, understands and loves the law *more* than someone who is seeking to be saved by it.

How can this be? Because although keeping the law as a means to salvation is null and void (and always has been, as he'll show in chapter four), the law has not been set aside or its requirements changed. The law of God is still there, and must still be kept. It must be obeyed for anyone to stand in God's presence.

The gospel does not declare that the law does not matter, but that it matters very much. It must be kept; and, for those who have faith in Christ, it has been. In order to be the Old Testament "sacrifice of atonement," which provided a glimmer of Christ's death, the animals used had to be "without blemish" (Leviticus 4:3; 16:3, 6-17). Why was that? Because the ultimate sacrifice of atonement, Christ, not only took his people's sin upon himself; he also **imputed** his law-keeping—his righteousness—to them. When we put our faith in Christ, our sinfulness is given to him; he has died for it. And Christ gives us his perfect obedience to God's law, and we live through

> The law must be kept; and, in Christ, it has been.

it. "God made him who had no sin to be sin for us, so that in him we might become the righteousness of God" (2 Corinthians 5:21).

So, the gospel upholds the law by demonstrating that law-breaking is so serious that it brings death and judgment; and that law-keeping is so fundamental that no one can pass through judgment without it being kept on their behalf. The law is upheld in Christ's life and his death, not nullified.

But isn't the law nullified in the Christian's life, if Christ simply imputes his righteousness to us? Not at all, as Paul would say! Outside faith in Christ, the law—when we allow it to speak freely and fully—is both beautiful and terrible. We love the picture of the perfect person we see there. Someone who forgives freely, blesses their enemies, is unfailingly generous, is pure in thought as well as deed, and so on is the kind of person we would love to be friends with. It is a beautiful portrait of what humanity could, and should, be. But it is also a terrifying standard, because every day in every way we fail to meet it.

So if you are obeying the law in order to be saved, you must do one of two things:

- Change the law, making it easier to meet its requirements. You want your commands to be limited and achievable. You don't want: "Love your neighbor as yourself;" you want: *Don't drink alcohol* or: *Go to church*.

- Be crushed by the law, because you know you cannot meet its requirements. You will either hate yourself for failing; or (as Luther did) you will come to hate God, because you cannot meet his requirements.

> Only the gospel allows us to recognize and uphold the perfect standards of the law.

Whichever you do, you will nullify the law! Only the gospel allows us to recognize and uphold the perfect standards of the law, because we know that the law matters enough to God for it to bring death; but we also know that it no longer means *our* death. We don't need to ignore the law we cannot keep, or be crushed by the law we cannot keep. We are free to have a right respect for moral absolutes and to care deeply about justice. We can be secure in ourselves, non-judgmental of others, forgiving to those who wrong us, and not crushed by our own flaws and failings.

The gospel frees us to uphold the law.

Questions for reflection

1. How do these verses change your view of yourself?

2. How do these verses change your view of God's law?

3. What, apart from Christ, might you be tempted to boast in as the grounds of your confidence or self-worth today? How will you ensure you boast only in Christ?

7. WHEN JUSTIFICATION STARTED

Paul has made his great claim of justification by faith in Christ alone—a faith which excludes boasting and upholds the law. Now he calls two witnesses to support his case—Abraham, and David. "What then shall we say that Abraham, our forefather, discovered in this matter?" (**v 1**). "David says the same thing" (**v 6**).

This is a masterstroke. Abraham was the father of the Jews. The nation of Israel began when God promised Israel's ancestor, Abraham, that he would make his descendants into a great nation, living in a God-given land, blessed by God (Genesis 12:1-3). And David was the greatest king of the Jews, under whom the nation of Israel reached its Old Testament high-water mark. And Paul, throughout chapters 1 through 3, has been opposing nationalistic, works-righteousness Jews. So who would both the father-founder and the model king agree with? That is the question of Romans 4.

Nothing to Boast About

The first possibility is that "Abraham was justified by works" (**v 2**)—that Abraham shows us that saving faith equals obedience. If this were the case, Paul continues, then the logical conclusion is that Abraham "had something to boast about." If faith equals obedience, then we who are saved would be able to boast before God and others, for we would be the real authors of our salvation.

But at this point, Paul throws his hands up at the impossibility of such a conclusion, because surely even Abraham could "not [boast] before God" (**v 2**). The picture is of Abraham standing before God and boasting about what he did, telling God all the ways in which he had obeyed. *Surely no one can do this,* Paul is saying.

And indeed Scripture proves that in fact Abraham had nothing to boast about (**v 3**). This verse introduces us to an extremely important word for the whole chapter: *logizdomai*. It is translated as "credited" (v 3, 4, 5, 6, 9, 10, 11, 22, 23, 24) and as "count" (**v 8**). This is an accounting term, meaning "to count as." To credit something is to confer a status that was not there before. One example is that some houses can be "leased to buy." I make payments that are rent; but if a decision is made to buy, then those past rent payments are now counted as mortgage payments. A new status is granted to those payments.

And in **verse 3** Paul, quoting from Genesis 15:6, says that Abraham's faith was "credited to him as righteousness." What does this mean? It is not merely that faith results in righteousness—though it is true that if we believe God exists, and that he deserves our obedience and worship, then out of that will flow righteous living. Nor is it that Abraham's faith was in itself a form of righteousness, meriting or deserving of God's favor and blessing.

No, this is something much more—faith *counted as* righteousness. It means that God treated Abraham *as though* he was living a righteous life. His faith was not righteousness; but God counted it as if it were. Douglas Moo writes:

> God treated Abraham *as though* he was living a righteous life.

"If we compare other verses in which the same grammatical construction is used as in Genesis 15:6 we arrive at the conclusion ... that the [crediting] of Abram's faith as righteousness means 'to account him a righteousness that does not inherently belong to him.'" (*Romans*, page 262)

Abraham was not in himself righteous, perfect and blameless; but God treated him as though he were. It is possible to be loved and accepted by God while we ourselves are sinful and imperfect. Martin Luther put it this way: that Christians are *simul justus et peccator*—at the same time both righteous and sinful.

The proof of this interpretation can be seen in Romans **4:5**, in the remarkably striking statement that God is a God "who justifies the wicked." Here is the truth that when you receive your credited righteousness, you are still wicked.

Justification and credited righteousness are therefore the same thing. To be justified is to receive credited righteousness. This is what Martin Luther called "passive righteousness," and what theologians term "imputed righteousness."

As Paul explains in **verse 4**, our righteousness is an either-or: either merited by our works, or credited without regard for them. When someone is given money, it is either as a result of his work—wages—or it is nothing to do with his work—a gift. Wages are not credited, given freely, because they are something that is owed, an "obligation." If salvation is not a gift, then God is obliged to save us, just as your employer is obliged to pay you. And that, of course, runs against the whole tenor of the Bible (including Genesis 15:6!)

What Saving Faith Is

In contrast to the model of "faith equals obedience," Paul gives us the formula: faith equals trust in God's saving provision. In Romans **4:5**, we are told that saving faith consists in:

(1) the ending of one kind of trust, and

(2) the beginning of another kind.

First, a saved person does not work (**v 5a**). This cannot mean that a saved person disregards the law (see 3:31). It must therefore mean that the saved person no longer trusts in obedience as a way to be saved. A Christian is one who stops working to be saved, not one who stops working!

Second, a saved person trusts God, who justifies the wicked (**v 5**). This means a Christian is one who trusts that God has a way to save apart from our efforts.

So saving faith is a "trust transfer." It is the removing of one's hopes and trust from other things to place them on God as Savior. **Verse 5** concludes by saying that if we stop trusting in ourselves as justifiers and start trusting God as justifier, the result is credited righteousness.

Even today, many Jewish commentators find Paul's definition of faith perplexing. One, Hans-Joachim Schoeps, writes: "Faith becomes [ie: is tantamount to] a zealous obedience in the matter of fulfilling the law … [Paul's position] of absolute opposition between faith, on the one hand, and the law, on the other … has always been unintelligible to the Jewish thinker."

Abraham Believed God

Abraham wasn't saved by just believing *in* God. **Verse 3** reminds us: "Abraham believed God;" he is the man of **verse 5**, who "trusts God who justifies the wicked." Saving faith is not believing that God is there. Further, it is not believing in a God who saves. It is believing God when he promises a way of salvation by grace.

You can have lots and lots of strong faith that God exists, that he is loving, that he is holy. You can believe that the Bible is God's holy word. You can show great reverence for God. Yet all the while, you can be seeking to be your own savior and justifier by trusting in your own performance in religion, in moral character, in vocation, in parenting, etc.

To say saving faith is a "trust transfer" is consciously to see where your trust is, to remove your hopes and trust from those things, and to place them on God as Savior in particular (not only on him as God in general).

In *Evangelism Explosion*, D. James Kennedy suggests beginning with a question if you want to share the gospel with someone:

"Suppose that you were to die tonight and stand before God, and he were to say to you, 'Why should I let you into my heaven?' What would you say?" (page 21)

Another version of the question would be: *Assuming for the moment that there really is a heaven, what do you think are the general requirements for admission? Who gets in, and who doesn't?*

Anyone who asks one of these questions to a random sample of church-going people will be surprised at the large number who say one of:

(a) *Because I have tried my best to be a good Christian.*

(b) *Because I believe in God and try to do his will.*

(c) *Because I believe in God with all my heart.*

This is not a trick question. It reveals common misconceptions about what it means to believe, to have faith. Answer (a) is a "salvation by works" answer. Answer (b) is a "salvation by faith plus works" answer. Answer (c) is a "salvation by faith as a work" answer. In each case, the person is religious, but is not someone who "does not work" (**v 5**); they have not done a real trust transfer. In the last case, the person has even come to trust in his or her trust! But each alternative misses the glorious release of the gospel. These false understandings of saving faith will lead to insecurity, anxiety, a lack of assurance, possible spiritual pride, touchiness to criticism, and a devastation in light of any moral lapses!

So this definition of faith cuts against both the religious person and the irreligious person. On the outside, one seems to have faith and the other does not. But the religious person may be just as lost, having never confronted his or her own trust in self-justification.

What saving faith *is* makes a total difference. If faith equals obedience, you are placing your faith in yourself and your abilities. This will lead to boasting and pride (or to despair and self-hatred if you fail). But if faith

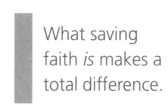

What saving faith *is* makes a total difference.

equals trust in God's promise to save, then you are placing your faith in God and his ability. That leads to humility and confidence—which is (as we'll see) what "Abraham ... discovered."

Blessed Forgiveness

"David says the same thing," Paul continues (**v 6**). David had many reasons to boast in himself: he was a king, had increased his nation's borders and brought peace, and established Jerusalem as his capital, with the ark of God's presence at its heart. Yet David also had many reasons to be crushed by his sinfulness: he was an adulterer, and, through conspiracy, a murderer (2 Samuel 11). And this strong, sinful man had discovered the "blessedness of the man to whom God credits righteousness apart from works." In Romans **4:7-8**, Paul quotes David's words in Psalm 32. Notice that David does *not* say: *Blessed are those who do not transgress, those who through obedience avoid sin.* He acknowledges he is a transgressor, a sinner—and yet he knows he is still blessed, because "the Lord will never count [his sin] against him" (Romans **4:8**). Being in a state of credited righteousness means that your sin is not counted (*logizdomai*) against you. Though you are sinning, it cannot condemn you; it does not affect your status before God.

Knowing the blessing of credited righteousness is the only way to be liberated to view yourself truly. Without it, we will either ignore the truth that God is righteous, and that he will only accept a righteous life; or we will be crushed by that truth. We will ignore, excuse or despair at our transgressions. But if we have saving faith, we can be real about ourselves, about our flaws and failings; and we can pick ourselves up when we do fail, because we know the blessing of being sinners whose sins are not counted against us—sinners who are righteous.

> If we have saving faith, we can be real about ourselves.

Questions for reflection

1. If God were to ask *you*: "Why should I let you into my heaven," what would you say?

2. How would you define faith? Has that definition changed through your reading Romans 4?

3. How do you experience the blessing of forgiveness? Are there things which cause you to forget or under-appreciate it?

PART TWO

Salvation, Circumcision, and Law

In **verse 9**, Paul is still thinking of the blessedness of forgiveness (**v 7-8**) as he returns to his discussion of what "Abraham ... discovered in this matter" (v 1). Is it "only for the circumcised, or also for the uncircumcised?" (**v 9**). The view he appears to be countering is that which suggests that Abraham's "faith" included circumcision. The Jews saw circumcision as the sign of membership in the Jewish nation. It was a religious and cultural symbol of belonging to God and of solidarity with the Hebrew people.

So if Abraham's righteousness was credited "after he was circumcised" (**v 10**), then it could be argued that Abraham "discovered" that there was an act (circumcision) on which his righteousness was based, and/or that righteousness was only available to the Jews, God's ancient people.

But in fact, "it was not after, but before!" (**v 10**). Abraham was already credited as righteous in Genesis 15:6, though he didn't get circumcised until Genesis 17. Circumcision was not a condition of him being reckoned as righteous; it was "the sign ... a seal" of what he already was, "by faith" alone (Romans **4:11**). It was the physical sign of the spiritual reality; and that reality did not rely on bearing the sign.

So, Paul reasons in **verses 11-12**, if Abraham was saved by faith without circumcision, then uncircumcised non-Jewish people will also be saved by that same faith, without circumcision. The chronology of Abraham's life is embodied proof of the principle Paul already set forth in 3:29-30—that God is the God of Jew and Gentile, and justifies both on the same grounds, "through that same faith."

> Abraham's life is embodied proof that God is God of Jew and Gentile.

In **4:13-17**, Paul again contrasts these same two models of faith. "It was not through law"—not through obedience—that Abraham was given the promise that "he would be heir of the world." How could it be? The "law" was given by God to **Moses**, around 500 years after Abraham lived and was saved. He could not have obeyed the Mosaic law, since it had not yet come. So how was he saved? Through trust in the promises of God.

In fact, the law *cannot* be the route to salvation. "If those who live by law are heirs, faith has no value and the promise is worthless, because law brings wrath" (**v 14-15**). If you live by law, you can't receive what's promised (because you are trusting in your wages rather than receiving the gift). If the promise rests on any kind of law-keeping, it is "useless"—because no one keeps the law (as Paul has already shown at length back in chapters 2 and 3). The law can only show us where we fall short, which is likely what Paul is saying in the strange phrase at the end of **4:15**: "where there is no law there is no transgression." Paul is not saying that if someone does not know the law, they cannot be guilty of sin. But transgression carries the meaning of a deliberate, knowing contravening of a boundary. If I trespass on private

> Knowing the law does not make us heirs; it makes us doubly guilty.

property, I am guilty of trespassing. But if I see a sign saying *Private property. Keep out* and trespass, then I am a transgressor: I knew the law explicitly, and broke it. Knowing the law does not make us heirs; it makes us doubly guilty.

"Therefore, the promise comes"—and *can only* come—"by faith, so that it may be by grace" (**v 16**). Because saving faith is trusting in the promises of God, salvation comes to us "guaranteed" (**v 16**), since it relies on God's promise, not our obedience—and it is equally available to Jew ("those who are of the law") and non-Jew ("those who are [only] of the faith of Abraham"). As in verse 3, Paul shows that his argument is proved by the Old Testament Scriptures: God promised to make Abraham "a father of many nations" (**v 17**, see Genesis 17:5);

as our father in the faith, he now has children throughout the world. Restricting the offer of salvation to Israel is to contradict the promises of God.

Abraham: A Case Study of Faith

Paul concludes his consideration of Abraham in Romans 4:17b-25 by presenting him as a case study of real, living faith, for us to follow as his "children." What does it mean to "believe God"? Abraham shows us it is to do three things:

1. *To know that reality is greater than how we feel or how things appear.* "He faced the fact that his body was as good as dead" (**v 19a**). God had promised him descendants (Genesis 12:2, 7), yet he had none: "he was about a hundred years old" and his wife "Sarah's womb was also dead" (Romans **4:19**). Elsewhere, Paul says: "We live by faith, not by sight" (2 Corinthians 5:7). Faith is not opposed to reason, but it is sometimes opposed to feelings and appearances. Abraham looked at his body and it looked hopeless. But he didn't go on appearances. This shows us that faith is not simply an optimism about life in general, nor is it faith in oneself. It is the opposite. Faith begins with a kind of death to self-trust. Faith is going on something despite our weakness, despite our feelings and perceptions.

2. *To focus on facts about God.* Despite the apparent impossibility of the promises being kept, Abraham "gave glory to God, being fully persuaded that God had power" (Romans **4:20-21**). This shows that faith is not the absence of thinking, but rather, a profound insistence on acting out of measured reflection instead of just reacting to circumstances. Abraham pondered and considered the power of God. He believed that the God who had promised him a child was "the God who gives life to the dead and calls things that are not as though they were" (**v 17**). We can imagine him reasoning it out: *If there is a Creator God at all (and I know there is), he must have all power—there can be no limit to it. God knows*

Sarah and I are both old, but he's the One who hung the sun and moon and scattered the stars like sand with both hands! It is ridiculous for me to think our age presents such a being with an obstacle! Faith is thinking about God, focusing on facts about him. We, of course, have far more facts about God to focus on, far greater demonstrations of his love and power. We know that God made Sarah's barren womb a place of life (Genesis 21:1-2); and we know that, supremely, he raised his own Son to life. We have far more to go on than Abraham did as we consider who God is, and what he is capable of!

3. *To trust the bare word of God.* Abraham believed "that God had power to do what he had promised" (Romans **4:21**). "Believing God" is not simply thinking about God, but trusting his word. Indeed, it is taking God at his word even when there is nothing else to go on—when feelings, popular opinion, and common sense seem to contradict his promise. It is to look at what God has said, and let that define reality for you.

Abraham shows us the way to strengthen our faith.

1. Get to know a lot more about God! Study, reflect, meditate. Abraham was able to overcome his sense of weakness by reasoning things on the basis of what he knew about God. You need to do the same.

2. Act on God's promises and word even when it is hard. Faith is living as if these promises are true. For example, you generously give away your money, though that may appear economically risky, because of his promise to care for the generous giver (Malachi 3:9-10). You tell the truth even though it may cost you a friend or favor with a particular circle, because you know it pleases the God who is Lord of history and who holds the hearts of all people in his hands.

Abraham's life also reminds us of what a real life of faith looks like. Paul says that Abraham "did not waver through unbelief regarding the promise of God" (Romans **4:20**). Yet a quick read of the account of his life in Genesis suggests that he did waver! He questioned God about God's promise (Genesis 15:2); he lied about who Sarah was (Genesis 12:10-16); more than that, he tried to bring God's promise of a child to fruition himself, in sleeping with Sarah's maidservant Hagar (Genesis 16).

Abraham did not always live out his faith, his obedience was not perfect, his trust fluctuated; but his faith was never extinguished. He hung on to God's promises even in his own flaws and failings—and as he did so, he "was strengthened in his faith" (Romans **4:20**). He was able to look at a mistake and say: *This has reminded me that my only hope is to trust in God's promise, and trust in God to fulfill that promise.*

The life of faith is not the perfect life; it is the life which clings on to what God has said he will do, and which sees struggles, joys and failures as means of increasing our attachment to the God who makes and keeps his promises. This is what the faith looks like which is, the moment we put our trust in God's promises, "credited … as righteousness" (**v 22**).

> The life of faith is not the perfect life; it is the life which clings on to what God has said he will do.

Paul's teaching is that those wonderful words in Genesis 15:6 "were written not for him alone, but also for us, to whom God will credit righteousness" (Romans **4:23-24**). What does saving faith look like for us? To "believe in him who raised Jesus our Lord from the dead" (**v 24**), and to trust God's promise that his Son's death and resurrection was "for our sins … for our justification" (**v 25**). Abraham's faith was in the promise of a descendant; our faith is in what God says one of his descendants has achieved. This is the promise which is to define our reality and shape our lives.

The Difference Justification Makes

In calling Abraham and David as witnesses for his case, Paul has proved that justification by faith began before circumcision, and before law—that it was, continued to be, and must always be a righteousness credited to those with saving faith.

As he has proved this, Paul has also shown several outworkings of being justified by faith, which he will continue to do in the next chapter:

- *No boasting.* Our righteousness is credited, received; knowing this leads us to give glory to God, and have a hopeful humility about ourselves (**v 2-3, 20**).

- *No cowering.* We know we are sinful, and we know our sins are covered. We do not have our sins counted against us—instead, we have righteousness credited to us. This produces the blessing of grateful joy and deep security (**v 6-8**).

- *A great identity.* We are included in the great plan of what God is doing in human history, as children of Abraham through having the faith he did (**v 12-17**). This produces a great purpose and an understanding of what we are doing in the world.

- *Complete assurance.* The promise of inheriting the earth—of enjoying eternal life in a renewed world—is of grace, and relies on God's promise-keeping power, not our performance (**v 16**). This enables us to live without fear of the future, and without despair at our failings.

- *Hope when hope is gone.* There was no hope for Abraham and Sarah—except the hope of God's promises, and that was all the hope they needed (**v 18**). We have no hope of eternal life except that God has promised that in Christ we can be made righteous. We can face the loss of things we enjoy, and grief when those we love are taken away, yet not lose hope or feel that life isn't worth living. The person who believes God can face anything and say: *I still have God's promises—and that is enough.*

Questions for reflection

1. How is having a hope that goes beyond all human hope of particular encouragement or comfort to you today?

2. Can you think of ways recently that you have acted in faith when it was hard? Are you being called to do so right now?

3. Reflect on the list of ways that justification changes us on the previous page. Which is most precious to you today, and why? Which most challenges the way you see yourself and your life, and why?

8. WHAT JUSTIFICATION BRINGS

Justification makes a difference. It makes every difference—not only to where we are heading, but to how we act and feel in our present, in both good times and (more surprisingly, and wonderfully) in bad. It is to these present benefits of justification that Paul now turns at the beginning of Romans 5.

Since We Have Been Justified

Verse 1 has a double introduction. "Therefore," Paul begins—in other words, these verses are the consequence of truths he has just been setting out. "Since we have been justified through faith"—these consequences will be the benefits that flow from the great doctrine of justification by faith that Abraham and David knew and lived by, and which was finally and eternally seen and secured at the cross. Paul is saying: *In light of all that we have seen, here are three realities that justification brings...*

First, there is peace with God (**v 1**). This is not the same as the peace *of* God (Philippians 4:7). The peace *of* God is a calm and satisfied heart in the midst of troubles and pressures. The peace of God is peace with regard to the cares of the world. It is **subjective**. But peace *with* God means that the state of hostilities between God and us is now over. Peace with God is peace with regard to God. It is **objective**, and happens whether or not I feel happy and secure.

"Peace with God" means that, until salvation, there is a war going on between God and us. When we disobey God, two things happen. The first is that when you sin, you not only break his law, but you assume the right or authority to do so—you claim kingship over yourself and your world. But God claims kingship over the same things. Whenever two parties claim absolute kingly control over something, there is a war. The second is that our disobedience means that God has a problem with us. It is not just that we are hostile to him. Paul has already told us that God's wrath is upon us (Romans 1:18). As we saw in Romans 1, God's anger is not the same as ours. It is not vengeful or vindictive; it is legal. There is a sentence on us, and it cannot just be discarded. The debt cannot be wished away.

This is why we cannot simply turn back to God, as though we on our side can do all that is necessary to be at peace once more. We need it to become true that we "were reconciled to him … [and] have now received reconciliation" (**v 9-10**)—that his anger has been taken away. Peace with God is not something that we achieve.

Second, there is "access to grace in which we stand" (**v 2a**). The Greek word here, *prosagoge,* has the sense of "to bring near," or "to introduce." We can only develop a personal relationship with a powerful **dignitary** if someone introduces us. Access to grace means we are given a favorable position from which to develop a personal relationship. In Christ, we are ushered into the royal throne room, and we stand—remain—there. Wherever we go in the world, we are always in the heavenly throne room.

> Wherever we go in the world, we are always in the heavenly throne room.

This goes beyond "peace with God," which was the ending of hostility. Justification is not merely the removal of a negative (hostility)—it has a positive aspect: relationship. This is friendship with God. We can now go to God continually with our requests, problems, and failures; and he hears us and relates to us.

Third, there is the hope of the glory of God (**v 2b**). This is a definite anticipation of sharing God's future glory. The word "hope" in English is rather weak. To "hope" means to want something without certainty. But the Greek word underlying it, *elpis*, means a conviction. Christian hope is not a hopeful wish—it is a hope-filled certainty.

The reason this benefit comes third is because the more we experience our peace and access with the Father, the more desirous we are to see him face to face, and the more certain and thrilled we become about the prospect of glory and heaven. By itself, "heaven" can be an abstract and unappetizing idea. But if you come to taste "access" with God and realize how intoxicating it is just to have a couple of drops of his presence on your tongue, you will desire to drink from the fountainhead. That desire, focus, and joyous certainty of the future is called the "hope of glory."

Notice that these three benefits of justification are the three tenses of our salvation. In Christ, we have been freed from our past (our old record of rebellion and sin is put away and we have peace with God); we are free in the present to enjoy personal relationship with God; and we will one day most certainly experience the freedom of life lived in the full, awesome presence of God's glory.

Joy in Sufferings

These are wonderful benefits—but life is complex, and involves pain as much as pleasure. When life is "up," we can savor and enjoy these benefits. But when things are "down," what difference does peace and access and future glory make?

Paul says: *Every difference.* We rejoice in our hope of glory (**v 2**); but not only this, he continues (**v 3**): "we also rejoice in our sufferings." In effect he says: *Not only do we have these joys, but these joys remain joys in our sorrow, and even help us to find joy in our sorrow.*

Paul does not say we rejoice *for* our sufferings, because that would be masochism. It actually is possible to rejoice for suffering: some people need to feel punished in order to deal with their sense of unworthiness and guilt. Others maintain a superior attitude toward people who have had an easier life. They see them as superficial or ungrateful.

It is also possible to use suffering as a work; as another form of justification by works! Some feel that God owes them his favor and acceptance because they have had a hard life. People who do not "process" their suffering through the gospel of grace can become proud and superior or deeply cynical.

Christians, however, rejoice *in* suffering. That means there is no joy in the actual troubles themselves. God hates the pain and troubles of this life and so should we. Rather, a Christian knows that suffering will have beneficial results. A Christian is not a stoic, who faces suffering by just gritting their teeth. Christians "look through" the suffering to their certainties. They rest in the knowledge that troubles will only increase their enjoyment and appreciation of those certainties.

What are these positive results of suffering? Remember that Paul is telling us how suffering affects a person who knows he or she is justified strictly by grace, not works. In that case, Paul says suffering begins a chain reaction:

1. Suffering leads to "perseverance" (**v 3**). This is a word that really means "single-mindedness." Suffering makes us "focus"—it helps us focus on what is really important. It makes us remember what really is lasting, helps us to re-align priorities, and so on. It removes distractions.

2. "Perseverance" leads to "character" (**v 4**). This is a word that really means "testedness." It is a quality of confidence that comes from having been through an experience. It only comes from following through and doing your duty despite it all. And the result is a growing poise that only comes from the experience. For example, a sports team new to the championship play-offs may play

poorly because they have not been in that position before. But a "tested" team, who have experienced the play-offs in previous seasons, will have fewer jitters. They perform well because they have been there before. Notice that without the first step, the second step won't happen. Suffering, if it first leads you to focus on God and proper priorities, will lead to greater confidence as you come through it.

3. All this leads to growth in "hope," which is a stronger assurance of and confidence in one's peace, access to God, and future glory. Suffering removes from us rival sources of confidence and hope; other places we might look to for our sense that, deep down, we are OK, and that our future will be OK. Suffering drives us to the one place where we find real hope, real confidence and certainty: God.

Paul's addition of **verse 5** right after verses 3-4 seems to mean that Christians who focus single-mindedly on prayer and obedience to God, and who therefore grow in confidence, will experience more of his love during suffering—an outpouring of love into our hearts. Many Christians testify that they feel more of God's presence and love during suffering because it makes them focus on and trust in him more.

Here is Paul's amazing assertion. When he shows that suffering starts a chain reaction that leads to hope (which is one of the fruits of justification), he is saying that the benefits of justification are not only not diminished by suffering, they are enlarged by it. In other words, if you face

> The benefits of justification are not diminished by suffering, they are enlarged by it.

suffering with a clear grasp of justification by grace alone, your joy in that grace will deepen. On the other hand, if you face suffering with a mindset of justification by works, the suffering will break you, not make you.

Consider how suffering affects people who are seeking salvation by works. Self-justifiers are always insecure at a deep level because they know they aren't living up to their standards but they cannot admit it. So when suffering hits, they immediately feel they are being punished for their sins. They cannot take confidence in God's love (**v 5**). Since their belief that God loves them was inadequately based, suffering shatters them. Suffering drives them away from God, rather than toward him. It is when we suffer that we discover what we are really trusting and hoping in: ourselves, or God.

Case Study

How does this make a difference to us, individually, in our own particular circumstances? Consider a specific difficulty or trial you have experienced as a Christian (it may be something you are experiencing right now). Take this as your own "case study," and ask yourself:

1. Did it lead you to focus, to single-mindedness? Did it help you sift out the unimportant from the important? Did it help focus your attention more on prayer and on what God has done for you?

2. Has your suffering produced testedness? Did you follow through despite your fears? In other words, did it bring a kind of maturity and confidence that comes from having been through it all? Are you a less jittery person, a less fearful person?

3. Did it lead you to a deeper experience of God's presence and love? Did you find a greater closeness, a sense of nearness?

If your suffering did not lead to this, analyze why.

Was it a failure of the will? Did you simply fail to spend time with God in worship and reflection? Or did you disobey him in some way to escape the hardness of the situation?

Was it a failure to understand the gospel? Did the suffering make you doubt God's love? That is a natural response, but did you eventually shake it off? The speed with which you do that is an indication of how well you understand justification.

Remember that God can use suffering to "awaken" a person to some sin—as a kind of "intervention." But interventions are only done by people out of love. God can and will treat you roughly if you need it, as a loving parent will do with a wayward child—but all out of deep concern. If you are a Christian, God has sent all your punishment onto Christ. All his wrath for you fell into the heart of Jesus and was swallowed up and absorbed there. It disappeared forever. He has no wrath left for you. You are free to view your sufferings not as God crushing you, but as God bringing you to a greater appreciation of the benefits you enjoy as his justified child. You are free to see suffering (as it is happening, not merely afterwards) in a way that only gospel faith produces: as something that does not touch your joy, for what you have lost in your suffering (comfort, health, wealth, and so on) was not where your joy is found.

Questions for reflection

1. How have you been enjoying your fellowship with God today?

2. Work through the case study questions on the previous page.

3. Is there an area of suffering or disappointment in your life which you are seeing as punishment from God, instead of God working to bring you closer to him?

PART TWO

Real Assurance

In **Romans 5:5**, Paul is (as so often in Romans) anticipating a question: *How can you really know this hope of glory is right? How can you know that you don't just wish it to be true? How do you **know** it is true?*

> How can you know this hope is right? How can you know you don't just *wish* it to be true?

Paul shows us that, as we see through the Bible, the Christian's ground of assurance is two-fold: one is internal and subjective, while one is external and objective. And both are necessary.

First, verse 5 tells us that we can know God loves us because of the experience of his love. "Hope does not disappoint us, because God has poured out his love into our hearts." It comes through the Holy Spirit. Therefore, every Christian has some inner experience of God's love. Paul's language shows that this can be quite a strong experience, though it can be mild and gentle too (which is more common).

The greater your inner experience of love, the greater your assurance, hope, and power. Generally the people who have most are those who are very experienced and disciplined in prayer, meditation, life balance and obedience.

Some Christians have experienced this assurance very powerfully. The early seventeenth-century English **Puritan** Richard Sibbes wrote movingly of the Spirit's work. Here is a paraphrase:

"Sometimes our spirits cannot stand in trials. Therefore sometimes the immediate testimony of the Spirit is necessary. It comes saying, 'I am thy salvation!' and our hearts are stirred up and comforted with joy inexpressible. This joy hath degrees. Sometimes it is so clear and strong that we question nothing; other times doubts come in soon."

(Original quotation in *Works of Richard Sibbes* vol V, page 440)

Or as his contemporary William Guthrie described it (again, I paraphrase):

"It is no audible voice, but it is a ray of glory filling the soul with life, love and liberty. It is like the word to Daniel that said, 'O man greatly beloved!' Or like the word to Mary [Magdalene, on the first Easter Sunday morning]. The Lord only said her name, MARY, and filled her soul so she no longer doubted she was his! Oh, how glorious is this manifestation of the Spirit!"

(*The Christian's Great Interest*, pages 108-109)

Second, **verses 6-8** tell us we can know God loved us because of the death of Jesus. It is a historical fact that "while we were still powerless"—sinners, and in our cases not even born—"Christ died for the ungodly" (**v 6**). God's promised King gave up everything—his own life—on behalf of people who had rejected him. Paul is making an argument we should all have clearly in our minds. It goes like this:

- **v 7a**: It would take a very loving person to die to save another. It's extremely rare that anyone would die in place of someone who is upright—though if they are also warm and kind and good, then it might happen. But even a very loving person would not die for an evil one. A very good one, possibly, but an evil or wicked one? No.

- **v 8**: So here is the single action which completely proves that God loves us. While we were sinners—part of a human race that was rebelling and resisting him—Christ chose, by the will of the Father, to die for us.

Therefore, Paul is saying, *you can know objectively and beyond all doubt that God loves you—even if your feelings or the appearance of your life circumstances might be prompting you to wonder.*

You Will Get There

Verses 1 and 2 could leave someone with the question: *I know that I have peace and friendship with God now, and that when I get to heaven I will have glory with God. But how do I know I will make it there? How do I know I'll endure in the meantime?*

In **verses 9-10**, Paul assures us that Christ's work for our salvation not only gives us hope for our ultimate future, but for our immediate future. We are assured that we will be preserved as "saved" throughout our life and through to the very day of judgment.

Paul's argument is very strong. He intertwines two arguments in these two verses. First, if Jesus stayed on the cross and saved us "when we were God's enemies" (**v 10**), then "how much more" will he keep us saved now that we are his friends ("justified by his blood," **v 9**)? If he was able to save us when we were hostile to him, would he fail us now that we are friends? If he didn't give up on you when you were at war with him, what could you do to make him give up on you now that you are at peace with him?

(God's wrath in verse 9 must be his future, judgment-day wrath, because Christians have already had God's wrath turned aside—see Romans 3:25-26.)

Further, if Jesus achieved our salvation when he was dead, "how much more" will he keep us saved when he is alive (**v 10b**)? It is not until the end of Romans 8 that Paul confronts the issue of "losing salvation" more fully. But here he answers the question indirectly. He says it is inconceivable that Christ should fail to save us to the end. As he will put it in Romans 8:32: "He who did not spare his own Son, but gave him up for us all—how will he not also, along with him, graciously give us all things?" The God who brought us into faith will keep us going in our faith. The God who opened heaven to us will ensure that we arrive there.

> The God who opened heaven to us will ensure that we arrive there.

The Joy of Justification

These first ten verses of chapter 5 present us with a wonderful series of the benefits justification brings. What does knowing the present and future fruits of justification produce in us? "We ... rejoice in God through our Lord Jesus Christ" (**5:11**), because we are those who have "received reconciliation" with God.

Joy is the great marker of the justified person. It is unique to Christianity, because it does not depend on your circumstances or your performance. When you give your heart to anything except God, and seek happiness there, you will be disappointed. You will, sooner or later, realize you're not that happy, or that your happiness is very brittle and in-

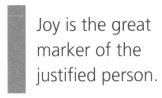

Joy is the great marker of the justified person.

secure, and you'll realize that thing can never make you truly, permanently happy, and you'll say: *Never again. I won't give my heart to that again.* But what do you do then? You will either look to something else, and be disappointed again, or you will give up on finding happiness, and become detached, so you can't enjoy anything at all. Ultimately, without the gospel we must either worship the world's pleasures, or withdraw from the world's pleasures.

But the gospel gives us God—and he does not change. As Augustine, the fourth-century bishop, put it in prayer: "You have made us for yourself, O Lord, and our heart is restless until it rests in you." We can find joy in knowing him, and knowing peace and fellowship with him, even if we lose other things dear to us. We can look forward with cast-iron certainty to our home in glory; and we can enjoy a foretaste of it—an *hors d'oeuvre* before the main course—as the Holy Spirit works in us to give us that subjective knowledge of God's love for us. Then, with our hearts resting in Christ—as we "rejoice in God through our Lord Jesus Christ"—we are able to enjoy all the good of this world, neither becoming disappointed by nor detached from it.

So how do we get this joy? Through knowing and living out and meditating on the doctrine of justification by faith—through loving the truths of these eleven verses. It is as we know more deeply what we have, who we are, and where we stand simply because "we have been justified by faith" (v 1) that we will find ourselves rejoicing in the certain hope of being with God, rejoicing in suffering, rejoicing in God.

The Signs of Rejoicing

What are the signs that you are rejoicing in God?

1. Your mind is deeply satisfied with the doctrine of justification by faith. You rejoice in it by studying it and speaking about it to others.

2. You only think of your past in terms of it. You don't say: *What a mess I made of it there!* Instead you say: *Me, a Christian! Despite my deep flaws, despite my record! Yet it is absolutely true!*

3. When you discover in yourself some surprising new character flaw, a fearfulness or a lack of self-control, etc., the discovery does not make you doubt God's love. Rather, it makes you feel closer to him, and his grace for you becomes more precious in your sight.

4. When your conscience accuses you and says: *How could God love you after what you've done?* you don't try to answer with reference to your performance. In other words, you don't say: *I had a bad day!* or: *I was under pressure!* You say something like: *Even if I hadn't done this thing, that would not have made me acceptable in God's sight anyway! Jesus died for me, and his blood can cover 1,000 worlds filled with people 1,000 times worse than me!*

5. When you face criticism, you don't say: *This is totally unfair.* You rejoice gently inside with thoughts like: *Well, I'm really a much worse sinner than they know, but…*

Well may the Accuser roar,
of sins that I have done:
I know them all, and thousands more:
Jehovah knoweth none!

6. When you face death, you do it with serenity because you are going to a friend.

Questions for reflection

1. Does anything make you doubt you will reach glory? If so, what—and how will these verses encourage you?

2. Where, other than God, are you tempted to seek joy? What do you need to remind yourself about God in order to rejoice in him instead?

3. Which of the signs of rejoicing in God on the previous page and this one can you see in your own life? (You might find it helpful to ask a Christian friend which signs they see in you.)

9. WHY JUSTIFICATION COMES

The second half of chapter 5 flows out of the first half, and introduces a comparison between two "Adams:" the first Adam of Eden and the fall, and the second Adam of heaven and the cross—Jesus Christ. In some senses, it is the ending and conclusion of this whole section on justification. Even by the standards of Romans, Paul covers a great deal in this short section! But it is very carefully crafted—as John Stott points out:

> "All students of verses 12-21 have found it extremely condensed. Some have mistaken compression for confusion. But most have ... admired its craftsmanship. It may be likened to a well-chiselled carving or a carefully constructed musical composition." *(The Message of Romans*, page 149)

It is useful to lay out the structure of this section before we begin, as a road map to keep in mind as we travel through. It essentially breaks into three sections:

1. **Verses 12-14b:** The career of the first Adam

2. **Verses 14c-17:** The career of the second Adam: how Adam and Jesus are different

3. **Verses 18-21:** The career of the second Adam: how Adam and Jesus are the same

Sin, Death, and Us

Paul has just confidently asserted that Christ has so overcome the barrier between God and us that we can have a certainty of glory. He knows this is a stupendous claim. So in **verse 12**, he is probably anticipating questions from a "realist," such as: *How can you make such a confident claim in light of the enormous power of death and sin now in the world?* or: *How can one person's sacrifice, as noble as it was, bring about such incredible benefits to so many?* or: *How can that one act really change my present condition and eternal future?*

> How can one person's sacrifice bring about such benefits to so many?

So in this section, Paul shows in great detail how Jesus' sacrifice could overcome evil and reverse the whole course of human history. He describes (in 5:12-21) the effects of sin in the human race in depths beyond what anyone would think. But, he says, the reconciliation we have in Christ can and will address the disaster of sin at every point.

Verse 12 presents us with a three-stage chain reaction. It describes three stages in human history up until the time of Christ. First, sin entered the world through one man: Adam. Second, death entered the world because of sin, as a penalty for sin. And third, death spread to all human beings, because all sinned. The order is: the entrance of sin, the entrance of death, the spread of universal death because of sin.

What does Paul mean by "because all sinned"? The verb "sinned" here is in the aorist tense. The aorist always points to a single past action. So by using the aorist here, Paul is saying that the whole race sinned in one single past action. To use a large collective noun "all" with such a specific verb tense is so awkward that it must be deliberate. If Paul meant: "all sinned continually and individually" (which is true), he would have used the present or the imperfect tense. William Barclay, the Scottish Bible scholar, put it this way:

"If we are to give the aorist tense its full value [here], and in this argument we must do so, the more precise meaning will be that sin and death entered into the world because all men were guilty of one act of sin."

(*Great Themes of the New Testament*, page 57)

In Adam

This is worth restating. Paul is not saying that humans all die because we are *like* Adam (ie: we sin like him), but because we were all *in* Adam (ie: when he sinned, so did we).

Verses 13-14b demonstrate Paul's meaning. In **verse 13**, Paul points out that between the time of Adam and Moses, God had not given out his law in a formal way. He then says: "But sin is not taken into account when there is no law." In Romans 2, we saw that there is real guilt for people who do not have the formal, revealed law of God in the Bible. Let's credit Paul with enough intelligence not to contradict himself totally here. He cannot be saying that the people who lived and died before the Mosaic law never had any guilt of their own. Why? Because they had the law of God in a rudimentary form, written on their heart (2:12-15).

Therefore, Paul is probably pointing out that guilt and responsibility greatly increase with knowledge and awareness. The people who lived before Moses were not breaking explicit commands (**5:14b**: "those who did not sin by breaking a command"), as the people after the giving of the law, and who knew that law externally and explicitly, were. The guilt of the people after Moses was far greater than that of the people before—but, Paul says, "nevertheless, death reigned" (**v 14a**). In other words, though the people were less guilty, they died no less.

We can put the logic this way: disease and death reign just as much over nice people as over cruel people, just as much over ignorant people as instructed people, just as much over infants (who haven't disobeyed deliberately) as over adults.

Paul is asking: *If death is the wages of guilt for sin, then why does death reign so universally, regardless of individual sin?* His answer: "As did Adam" (**v 14b**). He is saying: *Maybe they didn't break a command, but Adam did, and in him we are all guilty. We are guilty for what he did.*

As John Stott pointed out:

"We cannot point the finger at [Adam] in self-righteous innocence, for we share in his guilt. And it is because we sinned in Adam that we die today." (*Men Made New*, page 25)

Federal Headship vs Western Individualism

This teaching sounds strange—in fact, it sounds repugnant—to "modern," western ears. Why? Because we are highly individualistic. In the west, each man is an island—interconnected, but rising or falling, succeeding or failing, according to our own actions and decisions and abilities. We see humanity as made up of as many autonomous units as there are people.

The Bible takes a radically different approach—that of human solidarity. People of other centuries and cultures have been and are better at accepting this truth. Many other cultures accept the idea that the individual is part of the whole family, tribe or clan—and not a whole in and of him or herself.

The idea of solidarity is that you can have a legitimate relationship with a person so that whatever that person achieves or loses, you achieve or lose. This is the concept of a representative. A representative involves those they represent in the fruits of his or her action, for good or ill. In philosophy and theology, this has often been called "federal headship." The word "federal" comes from the Latin *foedus*, or "covenant." A federal head is a person who, through a covenant relationship, represents or stands in for someone else.

In the east today (and around the world in former times), it is considered legitimate for some people to have this relationship to you, either by birth or by assignment. In the western world, we only recognize the legitimacy of such a person if we voluntarily choose to be in that relationship. Here are some examples:

1. A representative in collective negotiation. If a trade union gives a representative the right to negotiate and sign a contract on behalf of the union, he is a "federal head." Or sometimes a head of state gives an ambassador the power to negotiate so that his/her actions bind the country to the terms of the agreement.

2. The power given to elected representatives. A national leader (or the legislature) can declare war. Even in the vast majority of the world's democracies, this power to declare war does not belong to the people. People do not vote popularly on whether to declare war. There are good reasons for this: such a decision could not be made fast enough, and sufficient information could not be distributed for an intelligent decision. So we allow and expect our representatives to act for us—and the consequences of their actions come to us. If our federal representatives declare war on a country, we can't say: "Well, I'm not at war with this country!" Yes, you are! If your representatives declare war, you have declared war. If they make peace, you are at peace.

3. When a defendant enters into a relationship with legal counsel. The lawyer represents the client in court, and has, literally, "power of attorney" to act for the client in various (and, for the client's future, extremely important) ways. This is how the theologian Charles Hodge described Christ's work for us as federal head:

   "The relation [of] Christ to his people ... is that of a [legal] advocate to his client. The former personates the latter; [he] puts himself in the client's place. It is, while it lasts ... the most intimate relation. The client [may] not [even] appear [in court]. He is not heard. He is not regarded. He is lost in his advocate, who for the time being is his representative ... He, not we, is seen, heard, and regarded."

   (*Princeton Sermons*, pages 48-49)

When it comes to Romans 5:12-21, the rub for westerners is two-fold. First, we dislike the very idea of someone standing in for us. We say: *It's not fair that I should be judged for what someone else did! I should have had a chance in the Garden of Eden myself!* And second, even if we grant that federal headship sometimes is legitimate, we dislike the lack of a choice of our federal head. What immediately strikes us as unfair is that we did not elect Adam as our representative. We had no say in it. If we are going to give someone "power of attorney" or "power of collective bargaining," we want to be able to choose someone just like us, someone who would share all our views and perspectives, but who would be highly gifted and able to represent us well.

But if we are thinking of it this way, we are on the verge of understanding how God did it! First, no one could choose a representative for you as well as God could. We must not think we could have made a more intelligent selection than God! And second, God did not simply choose Adam, he *created* Adam to be our representative. He was perfectly created and designed to act exactly as you, personally, as an individual, would have acted in the same situation. You cannot say: *I would have done a better job*, because that would be to claim that you could have been a better representative than God created, or chosen a better representative than God chose. No—God gave us the right, fair federal head in Adam. And so we are guilty in Adam because we actually sinned in him.

> Adam was perfectly designed to act exactly as you would.

As an aside, it is worth noting that often the people most offended at the doctrine of "federal headship" consider themselves very liberal and open-minded. Yet they refuse to detach themselves in any way from their furious western individualism when they approach this text. None of us are as detached from our culture or clan as many of us like to think.

Why Federal Headship is Good News

In fact, the truth that God deals with us in and through our representative is very good and liberating news. If we each had to represent ourselves as individuals before his heavenly throne, we would have no defense at all (3:20). Our sin would lead us to death. But instead, we are represented by Adam—we sinned in him, and our sin in him as our federal head leads to our death. Death reigned because in him all of humanity broke God's command (**5:14b**).

How is this good news?! Because if Adam's disobedience is our disobedience then, if there were an obedient man, a perfect second Adam, he would be able to be our federal head. He could represent us before the heavenly throne, and through him we could have the life that in Adam or left to ourselves we could never enjoy. It is wonderful news that God deals with us through a federal head—because "Adam … was a pattern of the one to come" (**v 14c**). It is because humanity is corporate, under a federal head, that we can, "through our Lord Jesus Christ … have now received reconciliation" (**v 11**). Federal headship means we can have a peace with God that the western individualism we are soaked in can never offer.

Questions for reflection

1. How would you sum up the message of this passage in a single sentence?

2. How do you react to the idea of federal headship?

3. As you look at your own life and history, in what ways can you see that Adam was a good and fair representative for you?

PART TWO

Adam and Christ: The Differences

Having said that Adam is a "pattern of the one to come" (**v 14**), Paul immediately clarifies what he does *not* mean by this! "But the gift [of Jesus] is *not* like the trespass [of Adam]" (**v 15**). Paul lists three contrasts between the two:

1. The motivation at the heart of each deed was very different. Paul calls Adam's deed a "trespass"—a conscious sin—but calls Jesus' deed the (free) gift (**v 15**). This means that Adam's act was a deed of self-aggrandizement, as contrasted with Jesus' act of self-sacrifice. In other words, Jesus' deed of dying for us was not simply obedience toward God; it was also undeserved compassion for us. Put another way, Adam's action was a breaking of the law, but Jesus' action was an "act of righteousness" (**v 18**) and "obedience" (**v 19**)—a total fulfillment of the law.

2. The results of the two deeds are opposite. First, Adam's resulted in "death" (**v 15**), while Christ's results in "life." Here is the first of the two consequences of evil listed in the beginning of the passage: physical death. The effects of Christ's deed undo the effects of Adam's. Second, Adam's deed resulted in "condemnation" (**v 16**), and Christ's in "justification." This is the second of the two consequences of evil listed in verse 12: legal guilt. Again, the effects of Christ's deed undo the effects of Adam's. Third, the result of Adam's sin is that "death reigns" (**v 17**); but Paul doesn't say that in Christ "life reigns", but rather that we "reign in life" (**v 17**). This is another contrast Paul is making. Before, death reigned over us and we were in bondage. Now we are free. The old kingdom within which we labored crushed us, but we have not traded in one slavery for another one just like it. Rather, in the new kingdom of Christ we become kings ourselves! Christ's kingship makes us kings, but sin's kingship makes us slaves. The contrast is total.

3. The power of the two is different. Paul is at great pains to show that the power and scope of Christ's work is far greater than Adam's. Twice he says: "How much more" (**v 15, 17**), to show us that Christ's work can overwhelm, completely cover, and undo all the effects of Adam's work. The contrast is between "sin," and "grace" or "gift." Our condemnation is an act of justice and justice metes out equivalence—exactly what is

> Christ's work can overwhelm all the effects of Adam's work.

deserved. But our justification is an act of grace, and grace overflows and abounds, giving us ten, one hundred, one thousand, and an infinity of times more than we deserve.

There is another, fourth, contrast between Adam and Christ that Paul does not mention in chapter 5, and which he will focus on in chapter 6—but it is helpful for us to mention it here. Our union with Adam as our federal head is physical, but our union with Christ as our federal head is by faith. God unites us with Christ when we believe in him. This is why Paul can later say "we died" with Christ, we "were ... buried" with him, and we "were raised" with him (6:2-4, 8). Until we are united to Christ by faith, all that is true of Adam is true of us. But once we are united to Christ by faith, whatever is true of him is true of us! John Stott writes:

> "So then, whether we are condemned or justified, whether we are spiritually alive or dead, depends on which humanity we belong to—whether we still belong to the old humanity initiated by Adam, or to the new humanity initiated by Christ."
>
> (*Men Made New*, page 28)

Adam and Christ: The Similarity

So, given these fundamental differences, how is Adam a "pattern" of Christ—how are they similar? Most notably, as we have seen, both stand for and represent a body of people, and what they have done (for good or ill) is transferred to those they represent. Paul uses several different words to get this across:

- **Verse 16:** One sin *brought* condemnation, but the gift *brought* justification.

- **Verse 18:** The *result* of one trespass was condemnation, but the *result* of one act of righteousness was justification.

- **Verse 19:** Through the disobedience of the one man, the many were *made* sinners; but through the obedience of the one man, the many will be *made* righteous.

One Man's Obedience

Verse 19 is worth reflecting on. How are we "made righteous"? "Through the obedience of the one man." Jesus' achievement was not simply to remove the penalty for our disobedience, wonderful though that is; it was to obey for us, as our representative head, throughout his life and supremely in his death. While Adam was told he would enjoy blessing if he obeyed God, and yet chose to disobey (Genesis 2:15-17; 3:6-7), the second Adam knew he would face agony and death if he obeyed—and yet he resolutely walked in obedience to his Father (Mark 14:32-36). When we read of Jesus' continual loving obedience in the Gospels, it is a matter of life and death to us; because that obedience is *our* obedience, if we are in Christ instead of Adam.

> Jesus' obedience is a matter of life and death to us, because that obedience is *our* obedience.

J. Gresham Machen, the founder of Westminster Theological Seminary in Philadelphia, put it like this:

"As a matter of fact, [Christ] has not merely paid the penalty of Adam's first sin and the penalty of the sins which we individually have committed, but also he has positively merited for us eternal life. He was, in other words, our representative both in the penalty paying and in **probation** keeping. He paid the penalty [of failed probation] for us, and he stood the probation for us … [Christ not only took the punishment by his death], but merited for them the reward by his perfect obedience to God's law … Those are the two great things he has done for us.

"Adam before he fell was righteous in the sight of God, but he was still under the possibility of becoming unrighteous. Those who have been saved by the Lord Jesus Christ not only are righteous in the sight of God but they are beyond the possibility of becoming unrighteous. In their case, the probation is over … because Christ has stood it for them."

(*The Active Obedience of Christ*, in The Presbyterian Guardian, November 10th 1940, pages 131-132)

This was no dusty doctrine to Machen:

"Recounted in the lore about the founding of [Westminster Seminary] is the stirring testimony of the dying Machen in a telegram sent to John Murray: 'I'm so thankful for active obedience of Christ. No hope without it.' Here was Machen's strong comfort in death. He knew that the meritorious work performed by his Savior had been reckoned to his account as if he had performed it. God must certainly bestow on him the glorious heavenly reward, for Jesus had earned it for him and God's name is just."

(Meredith Kline, *Covenant Theology Under Attack*, in New Horizons, February 1994)

Why the Law Came

Perhaps Paul is anticipating a further objection in Romans **5:20**: namely, that the giving of the law must have made a difference—that Paul should make room for Moses as another "head" of humanity, a humanity which has received the law. If this is the case, then Paul in verse 20 is agreeing that the law makes a difference; but not in the positive way this imagined objector might expect.

Instead, "the law was added so that the trespass might increase" (he makes a similar point in Galatians 3:19). When the formal law came through Moses, sin got more visible and it became worse, for now ignorance was no form of defense. Paul may have in mind the way we find that reading God's standards provokes us to think about breaking them (which he will explain in Romans 7); certainly, he is teaching that the law proves that it is not lack of knowledge which prevents us from obeying God and keeping his standards, but rather, lack of willingness and ability. We do not need to put in more effort; we need a rescue.

But sin, which the law points up, did not have the last word. We do not have to die in Adam. God's grace to humanity is greater than humanity's rebellion against God; "where sin increased, grace increased all the more" (**5:20**)—the English understates Paul's expression here, and a better translation would be "grace super-abounded." Why did grace abound in this way? So that where once sin had reigned and all mankind had faced death, now "grace might reign through righteousness to bring eternal life through Jesus Christ our Lord" (**v 21**). At the cross, we see the worst that sin can do, as humanity—of which each one of us is a part—crucified the Lord. But at the cross, we also see that the most that sin can do cannot thwart God's salvation. At the cross, grace overwhelms sin and life triumphs over death. The first Adam is not the last word for humanity. The second Adam, the perfectly obedient federal head, is. There is no hope at all without him; there is certain hope with and in him.

> At the cross, we see that the most that sin can do cannot thwart God's salvation.

A Doctrine Between Two Heresies

The end of chapter 5 marks the end of a section in Paul's letter, a glorious section which has laid out the gospel of justification by faith. The second-century church father Tertullian said that, just as our Lord was crucified between two thieves, so this great doctrine of justification is continually being crucified between two opposite heresies. The gospel keeps two truths together.

1. God is holy, so our sins require that we be punished. The gospel tells us: *You are more sinful than you ever dared believe.* To forget this leads to license and permissiveness—to what we might call liberalism.

   The doctrine of justification is crucified between two opposite heresies.

2. God is gracious, so in Christ our sins are dealt with. The gospel tells us: *You are more accepted in Christ than you ever dared hope.* To forget this leads to legalism and moralism.

If you eliminate one or the other of these truths, you fall into legalism or liberalism, and you eliminate the joy and the "release" of the gospel. Without a knowledge of our extreme sin, the payment of the gospel seems trivial and does not electrify or transform. But without a knowledge of Christ's completely debt-satisfying life and death, the knowledge of sin would crush us or compel us to deny and repress it.

So over the page is a summary of what we've learned about the gospel of God, between the two mistakes of legalism and liberalism:

Legalism	Gospel	Liberalism
God is holy	God is holy and love	God is love
Earn your own righteousness	Receive God's perfect righteousness	You don't need perfect righteousness
Matter is bad and we are fallen—be suspicious of or reject physical pleasure (asceticism)	Matter is good yet we are fallen—physical enjoyment is good, but live wisely	Matter is good and we aren't fallen—satisfy your physical appetites
Sin only affects individuals—just do evangelism	Sin affects both individuals and social systems—do both evangelism and social action	Naive about depth of human sin—just do social action
People can't change / change is easy	People can change, but there are no quick fixes	People don't need to change
Go into guilt—work it off	Go through guilt—rest in Christ	Go away from guilt—convince yourself you're OK
Repent of sins	Repent of sins and self-righteousness	Repent of neither

Questions for reflection

1. How precious is Christ's active obedience to you?

2. How have these verses caused you to love the Lord Jesus more?

3. Reflect on the summary table. What aspects of the biblical gospel have you learned that are new; or have you been reminded of that you'd forgotten; or do you now appreciate more deeply?

10. UNITED TO CHRIST

The gospel of "received righteousness" (as opposed to "earned righteousness") is radical. It says our moral efforts cannot contribute one bit to our salvation. This message is unique among world religions and philosophies.

Paul knows from experience that a question immediately comes up in any discussion of this gospel: if our good deeds are worthless for earning our salvation, then why be good at all? If the gospel says: *You are saved by grace, not by a good life*, won't that message leave the door open to immoral living?

So Paul poses the question of **6:1**: "Shall we say ... go on sinning, so that grace may increase?" Paul is asking: *Does the gospel message lead you to change the sinful patterns in your life? And if it does, how does it do so? Won't the message just encourage us to keep on sinning, so that grace will keep on covering?*

> If you are saved by grace, won't that leave the door open to immoral living?

In one sense, Paul's answer to this question is not a detour or a digression. Embedded in a critic's objection to justification is a fundamental misunderstanding of the doctrine. This is why Paul gives the (very short and simple!) initial answer: "By no means!" (v 2). That is: *You can only say a thing like that if you do not understand the teaching. If you understood the teaching of the gospel, you would not draw deductions like that.* In filling out this answer, Paul is basically re-explaining and re-applying the doctrine of justification and of our union with Christ.

Yet in another sense, this does introduce a new section. The objection of verse 1 leads Paul to discuss how the gospel does lead to a holy and changed life. Chapters 1 – 5 explain what God has accomplished for us in the gospel; chapters 6 – 8 tell us what God will accomplish in us through the gospel. These chapters tell us how to "experience" the gospel. They tell us how the gospel is dynamite that produces deep and massive changes in our actual character and behavior.

You Died To Sin

Crucial to the whole answer, and therefore to chapter 6, is the phrase: "we died to sin" (**v 2**). In understanding what Paul does mean, it is helpful to see what he does not. It is wrong, or inadequate, to say any of these things:

1. *"Died to sin" means we no longer want to sin; sin has no more power or influence over us.* But if this were the true meaning, Paul would not have had to write **verses 12-14**. If a Christian doesn't want to sin, why urge him or her not to? Also, 7:18 shows that a Christian still has sinful desires.

2. *"Died to sin" means we no longer ought to sin; sin is now inappropriate for the Christian.* The first interpretation goes too far; this one doesn't go far enough. Paul says boldly "we died," not "we ought to die."

3. *"Died to sin" means we are slowly moving away from sin; sin is weakening in us.* But the term "dead" that Paul uses surely means something stronger than that. Besides, the Greek tense used on this verb is the aorist tense, which refers to a single, past, once-and-done action. Paul is not referring to a continual process.

4. *"Died to sin" means we have renounced sin; at some moment (such as our baptism) we disavowed sinful behavior.* In itself this is true, but it is unlikely this is what Paul is teaching here, because

6:3-5 explains that this "death" is the result of our union with Christ. It is the result of something done to us, not something we have done.

5. *"Died to sin" means we are no longer guilty of sin; our sins cannot condemn us for they are pardoned in Christ.* Again, this is true, but again that probably is not the meaning here. Paul needs to explain why, given that we are indeed no longer guilty of sin, we seek to live without sin—why the gospel makes any difference to the way we live. Simply restating the truth that we are pardoned in Christ is not an answer.

So what *does* Paul mean? The rest of this chapter sets out his meaning in detail, but here it is in a nutshell: the moment you become a Christian, you are no longer under the "reign"—the ruling power—of sin.

> The moment you become a Christian, you are no longer under the ruling power of sin.

Remember, Paul has just said in 5:21: "sin reigned … so also grace might reign." In other words, sin still has power, but it can no longer force its dictates on you. In 1:18-32, Paul said that, outside of Christ, we are given over to our sinful desires. Previously, those sinful desires so ruled over us that we could not see them as sinful, and even if we did, we could not resist them. We were completely under their control. Now, however, sin no longer can dominate us. We now have the ability to resist and rebel against it.

There is a new power at work in our lives, ruling us: "He has rescued us from the dominion of darkness and brought us into the kingdom of the Son he loves" (Colossians 1:13). Or, as Paul put it in Acts 26:18, the gospel comes to people "to open their eyes and turn them from darkness to light, and from the power of Satan to God."

This illustration may help: If a wicked military force had complete control of a country, and a good army invaded, the good army could throw the wicked force out of power and give the capital and the seat of government and communication back to the people. But the out-of-power soldiers could still live out in the bush. This guerilla force could create havoc for the new, rightful government. It could often impose its will on part of the country, even though it could never get back into power.

So having "died to sin" does not mean that sin is no longer within you, or that it has no more power and influence within you. It does. But sin no longer can dictate to you. Though you *may* obey it and though (the Bible predicts) you *will* obey it, the fact remains that you no longer *have* to obey it. You have died to it; it can be dead to you. "How can we"—and why would we—"live in it any longer?" (Romans **6:2**).

How We Died To Sin

Paul now goes on to explain when, and how, "you died to sin." "Don't you know," he asks us, "that all of us who were baptized into Christ Jesus were baptized into his death?" (**v 3**). Paul is thinking of baptism in the mode of immersion. The Greek word *baptizdo* was often used to refer to being drowned or sunk, and thus had connotations of death. Yet notice that water is not actually mentioned here. Paul is referring to the spiritual reality to which water baptism points. Paul has already taught us (5:12-21) that we are in union with Christ. When we believe, we are united to Christ, so that whatever is true of him is now legally true of us. Since Christ died, and dead people are freed from sin, so we are freed from sin.

But our union with Christ doesn't stop there. Since Christ's death led to his resurrection and a new life, so in the same way our union with Christ will, and must, lead to a new life (**6:4**). If we believe in Christ, a change of life will happen. We will not live in sin anymore.

One fruit of union with Christ is certainty. Since all that is true of Jesus is true of us, and since he rose to new life, so we know that we are living that new life. And that new life points forward to the future state of perfect glory we shall enter, with him. "We will certainly … be united with him in his resurrection" (**v 5**). If we know that we are united with Christ, then we will know we are living a new life, no longer under sin's dominance—and we won't ask the question of **verse 1**.

Old Me, New Me

In **verse 6**, Paul introduces another fact about ourselves, in union with Christ, that we should "know." He says our "old self" has been killed so that "the body of sin might be done away with."

Paul's meaning here is a fairly difficult interpretative issue that divides even the best Bible commentators. There are some who teach that the "old self" and the "body of sin" are the same thing. They think that "[the] old self was crucified" means that it is dying slowly. But every other place where the word "crucified" is used in Romans, it means simply to be killed. Therefore, Paul is likely saying that the "old self" was killed in order to get rid of the "body of sin." Thus these are two different entities.

What is "the body of sin"? Some think it refers to the "flesh," the sinful heart. But later in this chapter Paul says: "Do not let sin reign in your mortal body so that you obey its evil desires" (**v 12**). So the "body of sin" is the body controlled by sin. This is not to say that the physical body is sinful in itself, or that physical desires are sinful as such. But sin expresses itself through our bodies; or it reigns in us by getting us to obey its dictates; and so Paul calls it a "body of sin."

On the other hand, the "old self" is dead and gone. So what is this?

> "'Our old man' is the old self or ego, the unregenerate man in his entirety in contrast with the new man as the regenerate man in his entirety." (John Murray, *The Epistle to the Romans*, page 219)

> "The vital distinction [between the 'old self' and the 'body of sin'] is the distinction between 'I myself as a [whole] personality' and 'my body.'" (Martyn Lloyd-Jones, *Romans chapter 6*, page 72)

A Christian's "old self" is gone completely. The old "ego," the old self-understanding, the old stance of the whole person toward God and the world—all that is gone. It has died—I died—and "anyone who has died has been freed from sin" (**v 7**). As a Christian, "I," my truest self, really seeks God and loves his law and holiness. While sin remains in me with a lot of strength, it no longer controls my personality and life. It is still able to lead me to disobey God, but now, sinful behavior goes against my deepest self-understanding.

When a non-Christian sins, they are acting in accord with their identity, with who they are. Why *wouldn't* they sin? But when someone is united to Christ, everything changes, because who they are changes. There is a new "me." When a Christian sins, they are acting against their identity. Why *would* they sin? Therefore, if I sin, it is because I do not realize who I am; I have forgotten what has been done for me in Christ.

Questions for reflection

1. What difference does dying with Christ make to your sense of identity?

2. Do you truly believe that you don't *have* to sin? What difference does/would it make?

3. In what area of your life is sin fighting particularly hard at the moment?

PART TWO

Death is Past, Future is Certain

Paul seems determined not to understate the importance of our union with Christ. **Verses 6-7** focused on what has happened to us because our death lies behind us, for we died with Christ. Now, **verses 8-9** take us to the implications of being raised in and with Christ. "We believe … we know" that the power of Christ's resurrection has triumphed and will triumph in us. Paul's logic is that if we know that we died when Jesus died in the past, then we can believe that we will live with him in the future (**v 8**). How? Because Christ was raised to eternal life—so "he cannot die again" (**v 9**). Death has absolutely no claim on or power over him. And since that is true of him, it is true of us, because we're united with him.

Verse 10 is therefore a summary of the section from **verses 5-9**. As John Stott explains:

"There are radical differences between them [Christ's death and resurrection] … there is a difference of time (the past event of death, the present experience of life), of nature (he died to sin, bearing its penalty, but lives to God, seeking his glory), and of quality (the death 'once for all,' the resurrection life continuous)." (*The Message of Romans*, page 178)

Dead, But Alive

The outworking of our union with Christ in his death and new life is that we must "count [ourselves] dead to sin but alive to God in Christ Jesus" (**v 11**). Why must we count—reckon, or consider—ourselves to be something that we already are? Because being "dead to sin" (ie: "no longer under the dominion of sin") is like a privilege or a legal right. Though it may be true or in force, a person may not realize or utilize the right/privilege. For example, you may have a trust fund put into your name, but unless you draw on it, it won't change your actual financial condition. The trust fund should mean the end of your financial troubles, but it won't have that effect unless it is used.

So we must "count ourselves" dead to sin because unless we act on this great privilege, it will not automatically be realized in our experience. We have to appropriate it, live it, enjoy it.

Here is a vital illustration from Martyn Lloyd-Jones that depicts our condition. It is worth quoting at some length:

"Take the case of those poor slaves in the United States of America about a hundred years ago. There they were in a condition of slavery. Then the American Civil War came, and as the result of that war, slavery was abolished in the United States. But what had actually happened? All slaves, young and old, were given their freedom, but many of the older ones who had endured long years of servitude found it very difficult to understand their new status. They heard the announcement that slavery was abolished and that they were free: but hundreds, not to say thousands, of times in their after-lives and experiences many of them did not realize it, and when they saw their old master coming near them they began to quake and to tremble, and to wonder whether they were going to be sold...

"You can still be a slave experientially, even when you are no longer a slave legally ... Whatever you may feel, whatever your experience may be, God tells us here, through his word, that if we are in Christ we are no longer in Adam, we are no longer under the reign and rule of sin ... And if I fall into sin, as I do, it is simply because I do not realize who I am ... Realize it! Reckon it!" (*Romans chapter 6*, pages 25, 28)

Intolerance and Progress

What are the signs that someone is "dead to sin" (**v 11**)—that they no longer "live in it" (**v 2**) because it no longer reigns over them (**v 12**)? It is easy to assume that the "reign of sin" refers to blatant, violent, obvious sins. But a life of outward morality, an interest in Bible study, and an enjoyment of religious duties may all be present while sin still is reigning! The sign is not outward morality.

On the other hand, some people believe that the reign of sin refers to any sinning at all—the sign is sinlessness. In fact, there is a statement in 1 John 3:9 that reads: "No one who is born of God will continue to sin." But elsewhere in the same letter, John says that no Christian can ever claim to be without sin (1:8), and we will see that Paul still describes Christians as having sin (Romans 7:18). Sin still has power in us.

So to "live in it," as opposed to being dead to it, probably means something like "to swim in it" or "to breathe its air" or "to let it be the main tenor of your life." Thus, to "live in sin" would then mean:

> Sin can only dupe you if you can't see it for what it is, or don't care about what it is.

1. *To tolerate it.* Christians may sin, but the sin grieves and repulses them. This grief and distaste are signs that sin does not have dominion. Sin can only completely dupe you if you can't see it for what it is, or if you don't care about what it is. This is what John must mean, too— that no Christian will sin knowingly and uncaringly.

2. *To make no progress with it.* Paul means that Christians can no longer "practice sin habitually" or "unremittingly" without diminishment. When Christians give in to sin, they cannot remain there permanently. The distaste and disease of sin drives them out again.

In summary, Paul is not saying that Christians cannot commit individual acts of sin, nor even that they cannot struggle with habitual sins. He is saying that they cannot go on abiding in the realm of sin. They cannot continue in it deliberately, without distaste or diminishment. They do not live in sin any more; instead, they are "alive to God" (**6:11**).

Free to Resist

Before you were united with Christ, sin reigned supreme. Now, the Christian is free from its control; but he or she can still cede some measure of power to it. We are free to fight sin, and free to win—in fact, we have been freed *to* fight and win (see Titus 2:14); but we must still fight.

> We are free to fight sin, and free to win; but we must still fight.

Paul's teaching is that, since we can now obey sin *or* obey God, we must obey God. He urges us not to do two things. First, "do not let sin reign in your mortal body" (Romans **6:12**). Second, "do not offer the parts of your body to sin, as instruments of wickedness" (**v 13**). Sin cannot rule us, but it is waging war within us; we are not to let the guerilla force of sin, that has been pushed out of our hearts but still fights hard in our bodies, seize control in any way by obeying the desires it plants in us. And sin is still waging war around us; so we are not to offer any part of our body (this likely includes our strengths and abilities as well as physical parts of our body) as its instrument or weapon.

But it would be a mistake to think that the main way we live our new life is simply through looking at sin and its desires and saying to ourselves: *Don't.* Our new life in Christ is about living positively and pro-actively—about *Do.* So Paul encourages believers to do two things, the converse of those things we are not to do any longer. First, "offer yourselves to God," to live with and for and like him. Second, "offer the parts of your body to him as instruments of righteousness" (**v 13**). God's kingdom reigns within us and expresses itself through us as we obey him.

Not Under Law

In **verse 14**, Paul switches his language. He repeats that sin "shall not be your master"—is not, and must not, be our ruler—and then we might expect him to say: *because you are not under its power.* Instead, he continues: "because you are not *under law*." Instead, "you are ... under grace." Paul is saying that knowing we are "not under law" helps us break the power of sin in our lives.

This is something we will deal with more in the next chapter, because Paul will go into more detail about his meaning in the second half of Romans 6, but verse 14 shows us that to be "under sin" is the same as being "under law" (compare 5:20-21 with 6:14). It tells us that our freedom from the law as a salvation system is what makes us free from sin's mastery over us. Why? It is only as we break away from works-righteousness that the power of sin is really broken.

We are righteous in God's sight. If we remember this, the motives for our sin will be undermined. Individual sinful acts have sinful motivations. When we ask why we are moved to particular sins, we discover that our sins come because we still seek to find our "justification" (our identity, our sense of worthiness) in other things besides God. Thus, to remember that we are completely loved and righteous in Christ undermines and saps our motives and desires for sin.

Need to Know

Through these verses, Paul has repeatedly said we "know" or "believe" (**v 3, 6, 8, 9**). This shows that any Christian who continues to sin or falls back into sin has failed to "know" or think out the implications of what has happened to him or her in Christ. How can we use this approach on our sin?

We need to realize that we are not to be stoics when it comes to sin: *Just say NO!* Paul is showing us here that sinning comes not so much from a lack of willpower, as from a lack of understanding our position and a lack of reflection and rejoicing.

So the key is to know, to remember, and to think like this:

■ *I am bought with Christ's blood.* If we remember that, we will not act as if we belong to ourselves. We owe Jesus Christ our lives and salvation, and we cannot live in disregard to his will.

■ *I have been delivered out of the "dominion" of sin.* This means that the Spirit of God is within us, and though sin may seem too powerful to resist, that is not the case. We are children of God, and we can exercise our authority over our sinful desires.

■ *I was saved by Christ specifically so I would not sin.* Christ "gave himself for us to redeem us from all wickedness and to purify for himself a people that are his very own, eager to do what is good" (Titus 2:14). All the suffering and torture of Jesus was for that purpose; any Christian who gives in to sin is forgetting that. We should ask: *Will I defile the heart Christ died to wash; trample on the very purpose of his pain; thwart the very goal of his suffering?*

Paul seems to be saying that if you can see and think about these things and still sin, it shows that you don't understand the gospel, that your "old self" was never crucified, that you are still thinking and looking at life the old way!

So we see that the gospel gives us a new and different incentive for godly living than we had when we were under the law as a system for salvation. When we were using the law to save ourselves, our motives for being obedient were fear and self-confidence. Now, however, we know that Jesus died for us so that we wouldn't sin. When we realize the purpose of Christ's death and as we think of it in gratitude, we find a new incentive to be holy! We long to, and we love to, be those who "offer yourselves to God," because we know we are "those who have been brought from death to life" (Romans **6:13**).

Questions for reflection

1. Are there sins you have grown tolerant toward?

2. Think of a way you struggle not to sin. What would it look like positively to offer that part of your body/character to righteousness?

3. How will you "know" more clearly and more regularly that you died with Christ?

11. SLAVES OF GOD

If we are not "under the law," as we saw in verse 14, does that mean we are free to live in any way we choose?

If the law of God is no longer the way we are saved, are we therefore under no obligation to live a holy life?

This is the substance of Paul's question in **verse 15**. Although the questions of verses 1 and 15 are very similar, they are not identical. In verse 1, Paul is asking very generally, "If we are saved by grace alone, shall we go on sinning?" In verses 1-14, he explains that the gospel gives us a new and different incentive for godly living than we had when we were under the law as a system for salvation. When we realize the purpose of the death of Christ as we think of it in gratitude, we find a new incentive to be holy. It is not fear and self-confidence, but gratitude and love. And as we've seen, Paul ends this section by saying: "You are not under law, but under grace" (v 14).

> When we realize the purpose of the death of Christ, we find a new incentive to be holy.

Verse 14 leads directly to the question of **verse 15**. If we are no longer under the law as a system of salvation, are we under any obligation to it at all? Can we do whatever we choose? Do we have to obey the Ten Commandments anymore? Paul is beginning to address an extremely practical question: what now is a Christian's motivation and understanding of obligation in daily living? For example, are Christians obligated to have a "quiet time" of daily devotions? Why does a Christian get up early in the morning to pray? What is the inner motivation that leads to self-control now that we aren't "under law," and so are not afraid that God will cast us off because of moral failure? It's a question with great practical implications!

Slaves to Something

As in verse 1, Paul gives a very simple answer to this question: "By no means!" (**v 15**). Why? Because being saved doesn't mean you are free from having a master. You can be either a slave to sin or a servant of God; but you cannot be neither, and you cannot be both.

This is the essential element of Paul's teaching in verses 16-22. There are only two masters, one or other of which all humanity serves:

v 16: slaves to sin   OR   slaves … of obedience

v 17-18: slaves to sin   OR   slaves to righteousness

v 20-22: slaves to sin   OR   slaves to God

Paul says first that no one is free (**v 16**). Everyone is a slave to something or someone! Everyone is offering themselves to "someone." Everyone lives for something. We "offer" ourselves as sacrifices on some altar. We are all serving some cause, some "bottom line," and that something becomes a master and we become its slaves. Here is a helpful quote from Rebecca Manley Pippert:

> "Whatever controls us is our lord. The person who seeks power is controlled by power. The person who seeks acceptance is controlled by [acceptance]. We do not control ourselves. We are controlled by the lord of our lives."
>
> (*Out of the Saltshaker*, page 53)

Paraphrasing this quote in terms of our text, we can say we "offer ourselves" to whatever we "seek" as our highest good in life, whether power or acceptance or some cause. Then we become "slaves" of whatever that may be. Thus, no one is in control of his or her life. We are controlled by that to which we have offered ourselves. Whether we call ourselves religious or not, we all have a god. We are all worshipers.

In fact, Paul says, there are fundamentally only two kinds of masters or categories of slavery. "You [can be] slaves to sin … or to obedience" (**v 17**). To be a slave of sin is truly slavery indeed, for it leads to death. To be a slave of God leads to righteousness—love, joy, peace, self-control, and kindness.

So Paul's main argument is this: anyone who wonders if a Christian can sin is ignorant about sin's enslaving nature. Put another way: a Christian does not have to obey the Ten Commandments in order to be saved, but a Christian does have to obey the Ten Commandments in order to be a free (and thus godly) human being. If you don't obey the law of God, you become a slave to selfishness and sin.

Compare and Contrast

It is helpful to see how Paul compares and contrasts these two slaveries in terms of their origin (**v 17-18**) and their development (**v 19**).

First, their *origins* are a contrast. The tense of the verb translated as "used to be" (**v 17**) is imperfect, which shows us that slaves to sin is what we are by nature. This slavery begins automatically; we are born into it. On the other hand, slavery to God begins when we are converted—when, "thanks be to God … you wholeheartedly obeyed the form of teaching to which you were entrusted" (**v 17**). Notice the four elements that come together to bring us into this new condition.

1. "Form of teaching" means that conversion begins with a body of truth, a specific message with a specific content that must be received. This always means the gospel.

2. "Wholeheartedly" means that this truth convicts and affects the heart. Before the gospel hits the heart, it is possible to have a merely intellectual or behavioral "Christianity," in which Christian ethical principles are followed superficially. But grasping the gospel changes one's "bottom line;" it shows you that you are "offering yourself" to power or acceptance, etc. (ie: sin), even if you are morally acceptable externally.

3. "Obeyed" means that once the gospel truth penetrates the heart, it shows itself in real life-change. There is an "obedience that comes from faith" (1:5—in a sense, chapter 6 is answering the question or objection that 1:5 might prompt).

4. "Thanks be to God" means that this whole process is due to God's grace.

So, in summary, slavery to sin begins at our birth. Slavery to God begins at our new birth, when God's grace enables us to embrace the gospel in the heart (changing our motives and our "bottom lines"), resulting in a total change of life.

Second, the *development* of slavery to sin and slavery to God are very similar. In **6:19** we see that each kind of slavery proceeds and advances. Neither one stands still.

So "you used to offer the parts of your body in slavery to impurity and to ever-increasing wickedness" (**v 19**). Slavery to sin results in deterioration ("ever-increasing"). This deterioration comes because the **imperatives** of the lords of our lives—the things we serve—are seeking to work out their wills in the world through our bodies. As we act out of a particular purpose, that action shapes our character and will so that it becomes easier to act in that way again. So offering our bodies to sin leads to impurity, and to an ever-increasing cycle of sin, or "wickedness."

> The things we serve are seeking to work out their wills in the world through our bodies.

C.S. Lewis has an interesting description of how slavery to sin develops in our lives now, and how it plays out beyond the horizon of this life:

"Christianity asserts that every individual human being is going to live for ever, and this must be either true or false. Now there are a good many things which would not be worth bothering about if I were going to live only seventy years, but which I had better bother about very seriously if I am going to live for ever. Perhaps my bad temper or my jealousy are gradually getting worse—so gradually that the increase in seventy years will not be very noticeable. But it might be absolute hell in a million years: in fact, if Christianity is true, hell is the precisely correct technical term for what it would be." (*Mere Christianity*, page 73)

Slavery to God works in the same way. Offering ourselves "to righteousness [leads] to holiness" (**v 19**). As we act according to the truth, our character and will are shaped into habits of holiness and righteousness.

Living our Reality

These verses also teach us how we can live out, maintain and enjoy our freedom from sin.

As in verse 13, "parts of your body" (**v 19**—ESV translates it as "members") does not strictly refer to our arms and legs, but rather all our components that can carry out a design or purpose. Paul says that "impurity" is a motive or a purpose; to "offer the parts of our body" to it is simply to "act out." Thus we see also that slavery to God is the result of an active effort on our part to "act out" what we know is true of us. "Offering our members" (or "parts of our body") means we are to act in accordance with what the Bible tells us about reality.

We must remember that **verse 19** comes after **verse 18**, where Paul tells us: "You have been set free from sin." As we saw in the last two chapters, conversion brings us into a new realm and puts a new power into us. Sin no longer can force us to do anything. So when **verse 19** says: "Now offer them in slavery to righteousness," Paul is saying: *Be what you are—be controlled in your behavior not by feelings or appearances, but by realities that the gospel tells you about.*

How does this actually work itself out? It means coming to daily situations and recognizing the possibility of treating God as my highest good and thus my Master, or of treating something else as my highest good and thus my master.

For example, if someone says something that makes me look bad, I will offer myself as a slave to God or sin at that moment. I could let my desire to look good be my master. I could let my heart say: *This is a disaster! I look like a fool! I have to discredit this person quickly! I must pay them back!* At that point, if I act out of this kind of thinking (offering myself to it), I will respond with bitterness, harsh language, and so on.

Or I could remember that pleasing Christ is my ruling motivation. I could have my heart say: *Well, this person has pointed out (albeit with a hateful motive) a flaw that I really should deal with. But fortunately, God is my Judge and he has accepted me in Jesus Christ.* If I act out of this kind of thinking, I will repent before God in my heart for what I truly am guilty of, and respond with a soft answer (as Proverbs 15:1 commands) to the person who made the point.

Questions for reflection

1. You are a slave to something. How will remembering this help you next time sin tempts you?

2. How would you use this passage to answer someone who says to you: *I don't like Christianity because it restricts my freedom*?

3. How would you use this passage to answer someone who says to you: *Why do you bother to obey God, if he already accepts you*?

PART TWO

Christian **conversion** is too wonderful a reality, and experience, to be accurately summed up and described in a single **analogy**. So Paul issues an almost apologetic explanation for his use of the slavery **metaphor**: "I put this in human terms because you are weak in your natural selves" (**6:19a**). We need help to grasp the wonder and implications of our union with Christ. And so Paul continues to make use of his slavery imagery. He has shown that the origins of slavery to sin and to God are different; as we have seen, in the rest of **verse 19** he says that the development of those slaveries are similar. Next, in **verses 21-23**, he teaches that their *results* are a total contrast.

Death Now

In a sense, being a slave to sin does bring freedom; but only from "the control of righteousness" (**v 20**). When someone says that they are rejecting Christianity because they want to be free, they are right only in the narrow sense that they're free from living in the way that will most satisfy and fulfill them; in every other way they are slaves. After all, Paul asks these Christians: "What benefit did you reap at that time from the things you are now ashamed of?" (**v 21**). The only answer that can be given is: "Those things result in death!"

How does sin bring death? Ultimately, sin brings condemnation and separation from God for eternity. But Paul is talking of a "death" that these Christians used to experience; a death that non-believers know now, as well as the one they will know in the future. He is referring to brokenness of life. Here's how that works: if you don't obey the law of God, you become a slave to selfishness, lust, bitterness, pride, materialism, worry, driven-ness, fear, etc. The specific enslaving sins depend on whatever particular "bottom line" you have offered yourself to instead of God. For example, if you are enslaved to approval, you will constantly experience self-pity, envy, hurt feelings, inadequacy. If you are enslaved to success, you will experience driven-ness, fatigue, worry and fear, and so on. Anything you worship besides God promises much, but delivers worse than nothing. It is slavery: a constant treadmill of seeking to grasp, or keep hold of, something which can never really deliver. The only benefit of idolatry is brokenness.

And so the results of slavery to God are a complete contrast. "The benefit [is] holiness, and the result is eternal life" (**v 22**). Again, Paul gives us a present and a future focus. People who "offer themselves" to obedience grow in the **fruit of the Spirit**, and anyone who is awash in love, joy, self-control, kindness and so on, experiences liberty now, and can look forward to enjoying it eternally.

After all, sin is a master who always pays, on time and in full. The wages he pays "is death" (**v 23**). Sin pays out what we deserve for our work for him. On the other hand, slavery to God leads to "eternal life in Christ Jesus our Lord." Paul's meaning here is not that, just as sinful works bring death, righteous works merit life. No, sin gives what we deserve, but eternal life is only and always "the gift of God." Serving him does not win us salvation—however good our service, we can only ever say: "We are unworthy servants; we have only done our duty" (Luke 17:10). But those who know they have received the wonderful "gift of God ... eternal life" (Romans **6:23**) have a new Master, a Master who offers the fulfillment of working for him.

Married to Someone

Paul now, in the first six verses of chapter 7, gives a second answer to the question of 6:15. Does the gospel leave you free to live in any way you choose? *No!* says Paul. *You can be either married to the law, or married to Christ, but you cannot be unmarried.*

In **7:1-3**, Paul gives an illustration of a basic fact: the law only binds those who are alive! Death breaks the law's power. Marriage is a binding legal relationship, but it is only binding if both husband and wife are alive—"the law has authority over a man only as long as he lives" (**v 1**). If either dies, both are freed from the law of marriage—they are no longer "bound" (**v 2**). In the wife's case, her husband's death is what makes the difference between another relationship she has being adulterous or a legitimate marriage (**v 3**); and vice versa.

In **verses 4-6**, Paul applies this to us. While it is the husband's death that frees the wife to remarry, in our case it is our death (in Christ) that frees us to "remarry." The analogy is not completely parallel, but the principle is the same. Becoming a Christian is a complete change in relationship and allegiance.

What an incredible metaphor—we are married to Christ! To be a Christian is to fall in love with Jesus and to enter into a legal, yet personal, relationship as comprehensive as marriage.

When you get married, no part of your life goes unaffected. So though Christians are now not "under law," they have every aspect of their lives changed by the coming of Jesus Christ. No area is untouched.

> We are married to Christ! To be a Christian is to fall in love with Jesus.

Being "married to Christ" is the final answer to the question: *Can a Christian live as he or she chooses?* No, because we are in love with Christ!

Marriage does entail a significant loss of freedom and independence. You cannot simply live as you choose. A single person can make decisions unilaterally but a married person cannot. There is duty and obligation. But, on the other hand, there is now the possibility of an experience of love, intimacy, acceptance and security that you could not have as a single person. Because of this love and intimacy, our loss of freedom is a joy, not a burden. In a good marriage, your whole life is affected and changed by the wishes and desires of the person you love. You get pleasure from giving pleasure. You seek to discover the wishes of your beloved and are happy to make changes in accord with those wishes.

So now Paul has given us the ultimate answer to how Christians live. We are not "under law," in that we don't obey the law out of fear of rejection. In other words, we aren't using the law as a system of salvation, a way of acceptance or access to God, a ladder up to him. No! Jesus' perfect life and death are the ladder up to God, and we are accepted in him.

Pleasing Christ

Verses 5 and 6 are the parallel verses in Paul's marriage imagery to 6:19-22 in his slavery metaphor. Married to the law and dominated by our old sinful nature, our sinfulness was "aroused by the law" (**7:5**—an idea which we will see Paul expanding on later in Romans 7). And so, with our sinful desires inflamed we "bore fruit" which (as we have already seen) led to both a present and an eternal "death." Conversely—"but now"—we have been released from our old marriage, through our own death in Christ (**v 6**). Married to Christ and indwelled by his Spirit, we "serve in [his] new way" (a theme upon which Paul will focus in Romans 8).

So does the Christian ignore the moral law of God? Not at all. We now look at it as an expression of God's desires. He loves honesty, purity, generosity, truth, integrity, kindness, and so on. We now use the law to please the One who saved us. So we are not "under the law." We are not married to it. We are married to Christ; we are seeking to please him, and so the law's precepts are ways to honor the One we love. They are now not a burden—we have a new motivation (love for our Husband) and obey in a new framework (acceptance on the basis of Christ, not us, fulfilling the law).

Someone might say: *If I thought I was saved totally by grace and could not be rejected, I'd lose all incentive to lead a holy life.* The answer is: *Well then, all the incentive you have now is fear of rejection. You are under the law. If you understand that you are accepted, the new incentive is grateful joy and love. That is the right incentive.*

We obey who we offer our service to. We live to please who we are married to. We were once slaves to sin—we obeyed it. We were once married to the law; controlled by our sinful natures—whether pursuing self-righteous religion or self-centered **license**—we lived to please it. But our death in "the body of Christ" (**v 4**) has changed everything, totally and eternally. We are slaves to God—how could we, and why would we, sin?! We belong to Christ as his bride, knowing he died for us—how could we, and why would we, not live to please him, out of loving gratitude toward him? It is the Christian's identity—the Christian's relationship to God—that is ultimately the answer to Paul's question in 6:15. It is knowing who you are in Christ that causes you to say, deep in your heart: *Will I live in this moment as though I'm a slave to sin, married to the law? By no means!*

Questions for reflection

1. Can you think of examples from your own past, or in the lives of those you know, of how slavery to sin is a kind of "death"?

2. How does the image of belonging to Christ in marriage motivate you to live in a way which pleases him?

3. What practical difference does this image need to make in your life today?

12. WARFARE WITH SIN

Romans **7:7** introduces another question: "Is the law sin?" Paul is anticipating that his argument in 7:1-6—that we were "married" to the law, but now have been freed from it by our death in Christ, and are now married to him—will lead his readers to wonder if the law, from which we needed to be "released" and which is now "the old way" (v 6), is in itself a bad thing.

What the Law Does

Again, there is a (very) short answer, followed by a (much!) longer one. The short answer is: "Certainly not!" (**v 7**). There is nothing wrong with the law of God. But we need to understand what the law is *for*.

The main purpose of the law is to show us the character of sin. That is the only way to understand many of the statements Paul makes in these verses; for example: "I would not have known what sin was except through the law" (**v 7**). But how does it do this?

First, it simply defines sin for us. "For I would not have known what coveting really was if the law had not said, 'Do not covet'" (**v 7**). This means that the very concept of envy/coveting is outlined by the law. Without that standard, Paul would not have understood that this is sin.

Second, the law reveals sin in us. "For apart from law, sin is dead" (**v 8**). This statement indicates that when the commandment of God comes to us, it actually aggravates and stirs sin up in our hearts, showing us not just what sin is in general, but how sin resides within us. Paul states this idea again in **verse 13**: "In order that sin might be recognized as sin ... through the commandment sin might become utterly sinful." Paul is describing a situation in which he found that the more he tried to avoid coveting and envy, the more the coveting and envy grew! As he read the law, sin in his life got utterly sinful, ie: much worse, and totally inexcusable. Then he could see his sinfulness and his need.

Paul's point is that the law cannot save us—that was never, and could never be, its purpose, because it was given to sinners; but it can and must show us that we need to be saved—that we are sinners. Unless the law does its work, we won't look to Christ. We will be in denial about the depth and nature of our sin. In other words, we need the law to "**convict**" us of sin before we can see our need for, or have a desire for, the grace of God in Christ.

How Sin Uses the Law

Paul is saying something more than that the law shows us our sin. The law, he says, actually aggravates or provokes sin in us. "Sin, *seizing the opportunity afforded by the commandment,* produced in me ... [sinful] desire ... when the commandment came, sin sprang to life" (**v 8-9**).

How does it do this? The basic answer is that there is a "perversity" about our hearts. "Perversity" is a desire to do something for no other reason than because it is forbidden. It is a joy in wrongdoing for its own sake. Paul's point is that until the command against an evil thing comes to us, we may feel little urge to do it. But when we hear the command, our native "perversity" is stirred up and may take over.

This insight is a door to understanding the very anatomy of sin—what it is in its essence. Augustine has a classic analysis of this point in his *Confessions*. He describes a time when he stole some pears as a boy, and then draws some profound insights from his experience:

"Near our vineyard there was a pear tree, loaded with fruit, though the fruit was not particularly attractive either in color or taste. I and some other ... youths conceived the idea of shaking the pears off this tree and carrying them away. We set out late at night … and stole all the fruit that we could carry. And this was not to feed ourselves; we may have tasted a few, but then we threw the rest to the pigs. Our real pleasure was simply in doing something that was not allowed. I had plenty of better pears of my own; I only took these ones in order that I might be a thief. Once I had taken them I threw them away, and all I tasted in them was my own iniquity, which I enjoyed very much."

(*Confessions*, Book II, chapter 4)

Augustine is saying that there is always a "depth motive" for every sin. When a person lies or steals or is impure or cruel, there is always a superficial motive. There is greed or anger and so on. But Augustine's experience of the pear tree (and his study of Scripture!) showed him that the underlying, ultimate motive of sin is to play God. Imagining himself speaking to God, he continues:

> The underlying, ultimate motive of sin is to play God.

"In a **perverse** way, all men imitate you who put themselves far from you … What then was it that I loved in that theft of mine? In what way, awkwardly and perversely, did I imitate my Lord? Did I find it pleasant to break your law … unpunished … and so producing a darkened shadow of **omnipotence**? What a sight! A servant running away from his master and following a shadow! … Could I enjoy what was forbidden for no other reason except that it was forbidden?" (*Confessions*, Book II, chapter 6)

We have a deep desire to be in charge of the world and of our lives. We want to be **sovereign**. Every law God that lays down is an infringement on our absolute sovereignty. It reminds us that we are not God, and prevents us from being sovereign to live as we wish. In its essence, sin is a force that hates any such infringement. It desires to be God. What was the first temptation from the serpent, in the Garden of Eden? "You will be like God" (Genesis 3:4). That was the essence of the first sin, and it is the essence of all of ours, too.

Therefore, since the essence of sin is the desire to play God—to have no infringements on our sovereignty—every law will stir sin up in its original force and power. The more we are exposed to the law of God, the more that sinful force will be aggravated into reaction.

Alive Apart From Law

Paul says that there was a time, "once," that he was "alive apart from law" (Romans **7:9**). He seems to be referring to a past experience, but there has been a lot of discussion about his meaning here. It is impossible for a Jewish boy from a devout family to have been "apart from law" in the sense that he did not know it or try to obey it. There would have been no time in Paul's unconverted life in which he would have been unrelated to the law. So almost certainly, "apart from law" meant he had never seen the law's real and essential demands. He had not realized what the law really required. He saw a plethora of rules, but not the basic force or thrust of the law as a whole. He had no understanding of holiness, of what it meant to love God supremely, of what it meant to love his neighbor as himself. Thus he was "apart" from the law.

What does it mean though, that he was "alive"? Paul probably is referring to his own self-perception. He felt he was spiritually alive—pleasing to God, satisfying to God. He is telling us that this perception of being "alive" was due to his ignorance of what the law really asks for. And so, "when the commandment came ... I died." That would mean that subsequently something happened to show him that he wasn't pleasing to God at all, but that he was under condemnation. In very graphic language, he says: *I realized I was dead! I thought I was doing quite well spiritually. I felt good or better than most—but then I was overwhelmed with a sense of failure and condemnation.*

What caused this change in consciousness? "The commandment came" (**v 9**). It is obvious that God's law had "come" into the world centuries ago, so Paul could not be talking about the commandment "coming" into the world in some way. Instead he must mean: *The* *commandment came home to me.* Although Paul already had a conscience, now the demands of the moral law really hit him hard. He came under what is often called conviction of sin.

Remember, this doesn't mean Paul had never before seen that he sinned, nor that he hadn't seen the commandment before. Rather, he finally realized he was "dead," condemned—lost because of his complete failure and inability to keep the law of God. He had been a proud Pharisee, sure of his standing before God (Acts 26:4-5; Philippians 3:4b-6)—until he read the law, and realized that he was a sinner, in serious trouble. To "die" in this sense means to see that you are a moral failure, that you are lost, and that you cannot save yourself.

Internals, not Externals

Romans 7:8 suggests that the commandment that "killed" Paul was: "You shall not covet." This is not surprising, because Paul had been a Pharisee, and the Pharisees thought of sin only in terms of external actions. They felt that as long as you didn't perform an evil act, you were not guilty of sin. This made it far easier to think of yourself as an obedient, law-abiding person.

But Jesus showed that all the Ten Commandments refer not only to behavior, but to inward attitudes and motives. The Lord said, in effect: *You have heard it said, "Do not murder," but that means we shouldn't be bitter or hate our neighbor either!* (see Matthew 5:21-22).

However, when you read the Ten Commandments as they are written (Exodus 20:1-17), you could easily look at them only in terms of externals and overt behavior. So you could easily tick them off and feel that you are "alive" spiritually. You could say: *I haven't worshiped an idol, haven't disobeyed my parents, haven't killed, lied, stolen, or committed adultery. I'm doing fine!* In other words, you can interpret the law superficially, seeing it only as behavioral rules that are not that hard to keep.

But in fact, you can only read the commandments like that until you reach the tenth. The last commandment is the one that cannot be reduced to an external. "You shall not covet" has everything to do with inward attitudes and heart issues. To "covet" is to be discontent with what God has given you. "Coveting" includes envy, self-pity, grumbling, and murmuring. Coveting is not simply "wanting," it is an idolatrous longing for more beauty, wealth, approval and popularity than you have. It is not wrong to want such things, but if you are bitter and downcast when you don't achieve them, it is because your desire for them has become idolatrous coveting.

Paul had never understood sin as a matter of inward longings and idolatrous drives and desires. He had never seen sin as essentially "coveting" against God, failing to love God enough to be content. He had thought of sin only in terms of violating rules. So what happened when he really read, and truly understood, the tenth commandment? He realized that these commandments, given to show God's people how to live in his world, "actually brought death" (Romans **7:10**). Why? Because sin, using the commandment, "deceived me" (**v 11**) by stirring up "every kind of covetous desire" (**v 8**)—and so he broke the commandment; he was "put … to death" (**v 11**). The flaw was not in the law—quite the reverse (**v 12**): the flaw was in Paul, the sinner. Externally, he may be very good; internally, he could not be anything other than a sinner.

Questions for reflection

1. Think of your own journey to faith in Christ. How do you see the truths of these verses in your own life?

2. How, and why, is it helpful to be reminded that the commandments are about internal attitudes before they are about external behaviors?

3. Are there ways you are tempted to have a pharisaical view of God's law, and of the Christian life?

PART TWO

All this leads Paul to pose another question: "Did that which is good, then, become death to me?" (**v 13**). That is: *Is the law a killer?* "By no means!" he answers; it was sin that killed him, working through "what was good" (ie: the law). Sin is the killer; the law, which is good, is its weapon.

Paul the Unbeliever or Paul the Believer?

In the rest of chapter 7, Paul talks of his experience of struggling with sin. Is he talking about himself as an unbeliever, or as a believer? This is a difficult question, and plenty of thoughtful people have been on both sides of this issue. Some believe that a believer could not talk as Paul does when he says: "I am unspiritual, sold as a slave to sin" (**v 14**). He also virtually confesses that he sins regularly, even compulsively: "What I want to do I do not do, but what I hate I do" (**v 15**); "I have the desire to do what is good, but I cannot carry it out" (**v 18**). Therefore, over the ages, many people have concluded that Paul is talking of himself as he was before conversion.

I want to make the case that Paul is talking of his own present experience—his Christian life. The evidence:

- There is a change in verb tenses. The verbs of verses 7-13 are in the past tense, but from **verse 14** on all the tenses are present. A natural reading would tell us Paul is speaking of his own "now."

- There is a change in situation. Verses 7-13 talk about sin "killing" him. He's dead. But from **verse 14** on Paul describes an ongoing struggle with sin, in which he struggles but refuses to surrender.

- Paul delights in God's law: "In my inner being I delight in God's law" (**v 22**), even though sin is nevertheless at work within him. Unbelievers cannot delight in God's law in their heart of hearts:

"The sinful mind is hostile to God. It does not submit to God's law, nor can it do so" (8:7). This categorically denies that any unbeliever can delight in God's law, so is a strong argument that **7:22** can't be the words of an unbeliever.

- Paul admits that he is a lost sinner: "I know that nothing good lives in me, that is, in my sinful nature" (**v 18**). Unbelievers are unaware of being lost and so sinful that they can't save themselves. In fact, even immature believers tend to be over-confident, unaware of the depths of the depravity of their own hearts.

So the evidence in the text points to the speaker being "present Paul"—a mature believer—though this is an issue on which wise, godly people have respectfully disagreed.

Law, Law and Law

So if Paul is talking about the experience of living as a follower of Jesus, what does he teach us? His meaning is made clearer if we realize that Paul uses the word "law" in three distinct ways in these verses:

1. Sometimes "law" means the law of God (as in **v 14, 16, 22, 25**).

2. In **verse 21**, Paul uses the word "law" to denote a principle: "I find this law at work." Paul means: *I find this to be a general principle—the more I try to do good, the more evil comes at me.*

3. In **verses 23 and 25**, Paul uses the word "law" to mean a force or power. "But I see another law at work in [my] members … the law of sin." Paul is saying: *In my heart of hearts—my inner being (v 22), my mind (v 23)—I delight in God's law. God's law is now the main power in my heart and mind. But there is another power within me—the power of sin. It is not the ruling influence of my heart, but it is still within me and makes war against my deepest desires for holiness.*

The Real Me

Paul lays out his inner struggle—experienced by every converted person—in **verses 14-17**, and then recapitulates it in **verses 18-20**, before summarizing it in **verses 22-23**.

On the one hand, we now identify with the law of God. A Christian can now see God's law as "spiritual" (**v 14**); can desire to keep it (**v 15, 18**); can "agree that the law is good" (**v 16**). None of this was possible before we were converted. Further, Paul says that it is in "my inner being" that he rejoices in the law. This is like saying "my heart of hearts" or "my true self." (Some translations render it "my inmost self.") Paul here is recognizing that we all are aware of conflicting desires. We have, in some sense, "multiple selves." Sometimes we want to be this; sometimes we want to be that. Morally, most people feel "torn" between diverse selves as well. Freud went so far as to talk about an inner "libido" (filled with primal desires) and a "superego" (the conscience filled with social and familial standards). The great question we all face is: *I have divergent desires, different "selves." Which is my true self? What do I most want?*

For a Christian, that question is settled, even though the conflict isn't. The law of God is our "inmost" delight, "the law of my mind" (**v 23**). Of course, Paul sees that there is still

> The great question we all face is: *Which is my true self? What do I most want?*

a powerful force of sin and rebellion within, but those desires are not truly "him." "It is no longer I who do it, but it is sin living in me" (**v 20**). A Christian has had an identity transformation. As we saw in chapter 6, a Christian—the true "I"—really seeks God and loves his law and holiness. Although sin remains in me with a lot of strength, it no longer controls my personality and life. It can still lead us to disobey God, but now, sinful behavior goes against our deepest self-understanding. Even in defeat, the Christian has a change of consciousness: the "I," the *real* me, loves the law of God. Sin, on the other hand, is "it."

Yet though the Christian loves God's law, they still have a powerful center of sin remaining within. It seeks "what I hate" (**v 15**). The unbeliever cannot keep the law (v 7-13); but neither can the believer! Many people are puzzled that Paul seems not only to characterize his present condition as one of struggle, but almost of defeat: "I am unspiritual, sold as a slave to sin" (**v 14**). But the reason Paul tends to cast things this way is because he is looking at his struggle from a particular perspective. Paul is emphasizing that in yourself, even as a Christian, you are incapable of keeping the law. Notice that he uses the word "I" numerous times. Thus he is saying: *In myself, I am still unable to live as I should.* Even though there is a new identification, love, and delight in the law of God, a Christian is still completely incapable of keeping the law.

Warning and Comfort

Paul's words here are both a two-fold warning and a wonderful comfort to us.

First, they warn us that no one ever gets so advanced in the Christian life that they no longer see their sin. This is the apostle Paul talking! If we ever perceive ourselves to be "over" sin, if we ever feel ourselves to be pretty good Christians, we are deceived. For the more mature and spiritually discerning we get, the more we see of the sin in our hearts. The more holy we become, the less holy we will feel. This is not false modesty. Even when we know and see ourselves making progress against many bad habits and attitudes, we will grow more aware of the rebellious, selfish roots still within us. The holier we are, the more we cry about our unholiness.

Second, we're being warned that no one gets so advanced that they don't struggle with sin. It is quite important to expect a fight with our sinful nature. In fact, just as a wounded bear is more dangerous than a healthy and happy one, our sinful nature might become more stirred up and active because the new birth has mortally wounded it. The seventeenth-century Puritan John Owen wrote:

"As a man nailed to the cross, he first struggles and strives and cries out with great strength and might [though] as his blood and [life energies] waste, his strivings are faint and seldom ... [So] when a [Christian] first sets on a lust or [sin] to deal with it, it struggles with great violence to break loose; it cries with earnestness and impatience to be satisfied and relieved ... It may have ... a dying pang that makes an appearance of great vigor and strength, but it is quickly over, especially if it be kept from considerable success."   (*On the Mortification of Sin in Believers*, page 30)

But this passage also greatly comforts us. It is typical, when we struggle with sin, to think that we must be terrible people, or very wicked or immature to have such wrestling. But Romans 7 encourages us that temptation and conflict with sin, even some relapses into sin, are consistent with being a growing Christian.

The Cries of Your Heart

This means that the Christian heart cries two things at once, as Paul does. First, there is the desperate cry of discouragement as we look at our own efforts and failings: "What a wretched man I am! Who will rescue me from this body of death?" (**v 24**). When we read God's law properly, and when we look at our own lives honestly, we can only conclude that we are "wretched." Without accepting this, we will never grasp the glory of the gospel. We will never truly appreciate the gospel of received righteousness. Only if our hearts truly cry at our wretchedness can we then know the hope and liberation of looking away from ourselves and to what God has done. Who will rescue

> Without accepting we are wretched, we will never grasp the glory of the gospel.

Paul, and us? "Thanks be to God—through Jesus Christ our Lord!" (**v 25**).

By his own efforts, Paul knows that he will fail. He may "in my mind [be] a slave to God's law;" but "in the sinful nature [he is] a slave to the law of sin" (**v 25**). And so in a sense, **verses 24-25** look both back to all that has gone before in Paul's letter, and beyond to what will come. There is no hope in ourselves for our salvation, nor our obedience. All we are and all we have done merits only judgment. For our salvation, we can only ever look to God's Son, dying on a cross for us, as Paul showed in chapters 1 to 4. For our hope, we can only ever rest in his righteousness, as we saw in chapters 5 and 6. And for our on-going obedience, for any real change, we will need to rely not on our own efforts, as chapter 7 has established, but on the work of God's Spirit, which will transform our lives and our relationships, as the rest of Romans will show.

We are "wretched." God is not. Through his Son he has rescued us, and through his Spirit he is changing us, so that we can enjoy him for ever. Thanks be to God—through Jesus Christ our Lord.

Questions for reflection

1. How does the reality of Paul's Christian life encourage you in your own life?

2. Why is it liberating to be able to be honest about your wretchedness, and certain about your forgiveness? What happens if we forget one or the other truth?

3. How has the whole of Romans 1 – 7 changed your love for Christ? Your desire to serve him? Your view of yourself?

GLOSSARY

Abraham: (also called Abram) the ancestor of the nation of Israel, and the man God made a binding agreement (covenant) with. God promised to make his family into a great nation, give them a land, and bring blessing to all nations through one of his descendants (see Genesis 12:1-3).

Analogy: a comparison between two things, usually using one of them to explain or clarify the other.

Ascension: when Jesus left earth to return to heaven, to sit and rule at God the Father's right hand (see Acts 1:6-11; Philippians 2:8-11).

Autonomy: the ability to make our own decisions without being directed by anyone else; to be self-governing.

Blasphemed: when God is disrespected or mocked.

Circumcised: God told the men among his people in the Old Testament to be circumcised as a way to show physically that they knew and trusted him, and belonged to the people of God (see Genesis 17). It was also a way of acting out their acknowledgement that if they broke the covenant, they would deserve to be cut off from God and have no descendants.

Cognitive: something that can be understood in the mind.

Commissioned: given a specific responsibility, appointment or job.

Conversion: the moment when someone for the first time recognizes Jesus, God's Son, as Lord, and turns to him as Savior.

Convict: convince of the guilt of.

Covenant: a binding agreement between two parties.

Dignitary: someone of high rank or position (such as an ambassador or a senator).

Doctrine: the study of what is true about God; or a statement about about an aspect of that truth.

Ethical: an action that is right, according to a set of moral principles.

Evangelize: to tell people the gospel of Jesus Christ. An **evangelist** is a person who does this.

Faith: whole-hearted trust.

Fruit of the Spirit: the characteristics that the Holy Spirit grows in Christians, including love, joy, peace, patience, kindness, goodness, faithfulness, gentleness and self-control (see Galatians 5:22-23).

Functional: actual, real.

Gentiles: people who are not ethnically Jewish.

Gospel: an announcement, often translated "good news." When the Roman Emperor sent a proclamation around the empire declaring a victory or achievement, this was called a "gospel." The gospel is good news to be believed, not good advice to be followed.

Grace: unmerited favor. In the Bible, "grace" is usually used to describe how God treats his people. Because God is full of grace, he gives believers eternal life (Ephesians 2:4-8); he also gives them gifts to use to serve his people (Ephesians 4:7, 11-13).

Hebrew: a Jew, a member of Israel.

Imperatives: commands, or orders.

Imputed: a giving or sharing of a quality (either good or bad) to, or with, someone else, so that that quality is completely credited to them.

Kingdom of God: life under Jesus Christ's perfect rule. We enter God's kingdom when we turn to his Son, Jesus, in repentance and faith; we will enjoy the kingdom fully when Jesus returns to this world and establishes his kingdom over the whole earth.

Law: God's standards, given throughout the Bible; however, "law" often refers to the law God gave to Moses for God's Old Testament people, Israel, to obey (including the Ten Commandments, see Exodus 20:1-17).

Liberals: professing Christians who do not view Scripture as without error.

Licentious/License: living according to feeling, rather than principles, particularly with regard to sex.

Liturgy: a form of public worship; the order and language of a church service.

Metaphor: an image which is used to explain something, but which is not to be taken literally (eg: "The news was a dagger to his heart").

Moses: the leader of God's people at the time when God brought them out of slavery in Egypt. God communicated his law (including the Ten Commandments) through Moses, and under Moses' leadership God guided them toward the land he had promised to give them.

Mystical: non-physical, spiritual.

Non-sequiturs: a conclusion that doesn't flow from the argument made in support of it.

Objective: a truth which is based on facts, not feelings, eg: "I am married to this woman."

Omnipotence: the truth that God is completely all-powerful.

Orthodoxy: standard, accepted Christian teaching.

Pagans: people who don't know and worship the true God.

Perverse: something (a desire or action) that is completely wrong.

Pharisee: leaders of a first-century Jewish sect who were extremely strict about keeping God's laws externally, and who added extra laws around God's law, to ensure that they wouldn't break it.

Probation: a period of testing or observation of someone's qualities, where a satisfactory performance will lead to some form of reward.

Professing: someone who claims to be something (eg: a professing Christian is anyone who says they are a Christian).

Puritan: a member of a sixteenth and seventeenth-century movement in Great Britain which was committed to the Bible as God's word, to simpler worship services, to greater commitment and devotion to following Christ, and increasingly to resisting the institutional church's hierarchical structures. Many emigrated to what would become the US, and were a strong influence on the church in most of the early colonies.

Reformer: one of the first two generations of people in the fifteenth and early-sixteenth centuries who preached the gospel of justification by faith, and opposed the Pope and the Roman church.

Repentance: literally, a military word meaning "about turn." Used to mean turning around to live the opposite way to previously.

Sermon on the Mount: the term used to describe a sermon Jesus gave to a huge crowd on a mountainside, which Matthew recounts in Matthew 5 – 7.

Sovereign: royal, all-powerful.

Subjective: something which is based on feelings and opinions. Eg: "She is the most beautiful woman in the world" is a subjective opinion.

Works: things that we do, or achieve.

Worldview: the beliefs we hold in an attempt to make sense of the world as we experience it, and which direct how we live in it. Everyone has a world-view.

Zeal: great passion; uncompromising commitment to and enthusiasm about something.

APPENDIX: A Summary of Romans 1 - 7

1:1-7   Paul's life work: the gospel

v 1   The gospel is what Paul's whole life is about

v 2   The gospel is what the whole Bible (Old Testament) is about

v 3-4   The gospel is about Jesus, the God-man

v 5-6   The gospel leads to obedience through faith

v 7   Greetings!

1:8-15 Paul's goal: to preach the gospel at Rome

v 8-10   Paul wants to come to Rome

v 11-15   Though they are Christians, Paul expects to bless them by preaching the gospel to them too

1:16-17 Paul's thesis: the gospel in a nutshell

The characteristics of the gospel

v 16a   The gospel destroys shame (its effect)

v 16b   The gospel is a living force (its power)

v 16c   The gospel can save anyone (its scope)

v 16c   The gospel saves only those who believe (its condition)

v 16d   The gospel came to the Jew first, then the Gentile (its history)

The content of the gospel

v 17a   God reveals his perfect righteousness-record and provides it for us

v 17b   God's righteousness is received by faith permanently and exclusively

v 17c   Receiving it results in a new way of life

1:18   God's wrath: revealed and deserved

v 18a   Revealed: the presence of God's wrath in the world now v 18b   Deserved: we know the truth but suppress it to live as we wish

1:19-25 God's wrath deserved—we are "without excuse"

God discloses his glory

v 19   God's existence is plainly disclosed

v 20   God's nature (power and divinity) is revealed in the created order

Humanity rejects true worship and glory

v 21a   Refusal to glorify or thank the Creator

v 21b   True reasoning processes and unconfused emotions are lost

Humanity constructs a counterfeit worship and glory

v 22-23   Counterfeit religions and ideologies all worship something created

v 24   Counterfeit worship leads to bondage and addiction ("gave them up")

v 25a   Counterfeit worship is based on believing a particular set of lies

v 25b   Summary: if we won't worship the Creator, we will worship something created

1:26-32 God's wrath revealed—"received ... the due penalty"

v 26a   The principle of God's wrath: he gives us up to our false worship

v 26b-27   The effects of God's wrath on the desires

v 28-32   The effects of God's wrath on the mind and will

2:1-3   We are judged according to our knowledge (Part 1)

v 1   To judge someone brings a double condemnation (both the judge's and yours). Why?

v 2   God's judgment is totally just

v 3   We will be judged by the same standards we place on others; so moral and religious people are self-judging

2:4-5   We are judged according to God's patience

v 4   God never gives us what we deserve, but tries to lead us to repentance through blessing us

v 5   But God's patience will lead to greater judgment in the end if we reject him

2:6-8   We are judged according to our works

v 6   The principle

v 7   Eternal life comes to those who are glory-seeking

v 8   Wrath comes to those who are self-seeking

2:9-11   We are not judged according to our pedigree

v 9   Trouble to self-seekers, regardless of background

v 10   Honor to glory-seekers, regardless of background

v 11   God is an impartial judge

2:12-16 We are judged according to our knowledge (Part 2)

v 12-13 We are judged by God's law only if we have it

v 14-15 Those without the law are judged by what they intuitively know of it in the conscience

v 16   Jesus will be the judge

2:17-29 The failure of religion and moralism

The confidence of the moralists

v 17a   They have God's law

v 17b   They have a relationship to God

v 18   They learn and approve his will

v 19-20 They instruct and teach others in it

The failure of the moralists

v 21   They steal

v 22a   They commit adultery

v 22b   They have idols

v 23   Therefore they are hypocrites

v 24   Summary: moralism can't fulfill (and thus blasphemes) the very law it honors

The failure of religion

v 25   Outward observance without inward reality is empty

v 26   The inward is what counts

v 27-29 Summary: religion can't change the heart; and a changed heart is true spirituality

3:1-8   Answers to objections

v 1   Q: Paul, are you saying there is no advantage to biblical religion?

v 2   A: No, I'm not. There is great value in having and knowing the word ("oracles") of God

v 3a   Q: But then hasn't the word failed, for so many Jews haven't believed the gospel?

v 3b-4 A: No; despite their failure to believe, God's promises to save advance. Our faithlessness only reveals how true he is!

v 5   Q: But if he is faithful in response to our faithlessness, how could he judge anyone?

v 6-7   A: He will judge unbelief. That is being faithful in response to our faithlessness

v 8   Anyone who says (and I don't) that you can sin so God will love you is worthy of that judgment

3:9-18   Everyone is "under sin"

v 9-10 Conclusion: all are under sin's power—no one is right with God

Sin and our selves

v 11   No one wants God—all sin in the mind and heart

v 12   No one obeys God—all sin in the will

Sin and our neighbors

v 13   Sin and words: no truth

v 14   Sin and words: no love

v 15-17 Sin and deeds: we fight

Sin and our God

v 18   No one fears God

3:19-20 Everyone is under the guilt of sin

v 19   There is universal accountability

v 20a   There is universal condemnation

v 20b   The law cannot save us; it only shows us our condemnation

3:21-24 How the revealed righteousness from God is received

v 21   It is not based on keeping the law

v 22   It is received through faith in Jesus Christ

v 22b-23 It is needed by and available to every person

v 24   It is free to us but costly to Christ

3:25-31 How revealed righteousness from God is provided

v 25   It is based on Christ's death

v 26   It satisfies both God's justice and love

v 27-28 It gives all glory to God

v 29-30 It shows God to be God of the whole world

v 31   It satisfies the law of God

4:1-8   Why Abraham was saved

Abraham was given ("credited") righteousness, so salvation is a gift, not earned

v 1   He discovered justification by grace long ago

v 2   If he had been saved by works, he would have been able to boast before God—but this is an impossibility...

v 3   ... as Scripture says: he was "credited" righteousness

v 4   A wage is an obligation: a gift is not. Every benefit is either one or the other v 5   So salvation comes only to those who stop trying to work for it, but instead receive it as a gift

v 6   David also talks of this "credited righteousness"

v 7-8   A believer is one whose sins are not credited or counted against them

4:9-17 When Abraham was saved

Abraham's righteousness came before circumcision and the law, so salvation is for all, not some

v 9   Is this credited righteousness only for the Jews?

v 10   Abraham got credited righteousness before he was circumcised

v 11   Therefore, non-Jews who trust in the same promises will get credited righteousness...

v 12   ... and Jews who trust God's promises will get the same

v 13   Abraham got credited righteousness before the law was given

v 14   To live by law means you can't receive what's promised, and you only get God's disapproval...

v 15   ... for the law can only show us where we fall short

v 16   So salvation comes by grace to those who believe the promise, whether Jew or Gentile...

v 17   ... as Scripture says: he fathers not one but many nations

4:18-25 How Abraham was saved

Abraham's faith is a case study for us, so we can truly be his "children"

v 18   Faith's object: the promise of descendants

v 19   Faith's realism: he didn't deny the obstacles

v 20-21 Faith's focus: the glory and power of the promiser

v 22   Faith's result: credited righteousness

v 23-24 Scripture makes his faith an example for us

v 25   Our faith's object: Jesus (Abraham's descendant), who died and rose for our salvation

5:1-8   The benefits of justification we have now

Their description

v 1   Peace with God

v 2a   Access to grace in which we stand

v 2b   Hope of glory

v 3a   Joy within suffering

Their growth: through suffering

v 3b   Suffering makes the justified person more single-mindedly persistent

v 4a   Single-minded persistence produces confidence

Their growth: through experience of God

v 4b   This all leads to growth in our hope…

v 5   … which deepens through experience of God's love through the Spirit

Their source

v 6   Christ died when we were meritless

v 7   The most loving person would not die for an evil person, but…

v 8   … that is exactly what Christ did

5:9-11   The benefits of justification we will have later

v 9   If Christ died for us, he can "keep us saved" even through the judgment day.

v 10a   For if he died for us when we were his enemies, shall he do less for us as his friends?

v 10b   And if he saved us in dying, surely he will keep us safe as he now is living

v 11   So we rejoice now in light of the future

5:12-14b The career of the first Adam

We sinned in Adam

v 12a   Death only comes to those who are sinners

v 12b   So we all die because we all sinned when Adam sinned

We sin without Adam

v 13a   Sin existed from Adam to Moses before the formal law/Ten Commandments were given

v 13b   People without the law are not as guilty of sin as those with the law...

v 14a   ... but people died just as much before Moses...

v 14b   ... therefore people died for the guilt of Adam's sin.

5:14c-21 The career of the second Adam

How Adam and Christ are different

v 14c   Adam's action is a "type" of Christ's

v 15   The salvation brought by one man is much more than the sin brought by one man

v 16   Christ not only covers the guilt of Adam's sin, but all other sins too

v 17   Justice metes out equivalence, but grace overflows beyond what is deserved

How Adam and Christ are the same

v 18   As Adam's sin brought us guilt, so Christ's obedience brings us righteousness

v 19   More specifically: Adam's one act made us legally sinners (before we act), so Christ's one act makes us legally righteous (before we act)

v 20   When the formal law came with Moses, sin got more visible and worse, but...

v 21   ... when Christ came, grace arrived to overwhelm, resulting in eternal life

6:1   The first question (of four)

v 1   Does the message of salvation by grace alone lead you to stay unchanged morally?

6:2-10   Answer Part One: No, the gospel gives you knowledge of your new status with regard to sin

v 2   We died to sin when we became Christians

v 3-5   "We know" that when we were baptized with Christ, we died with him so we could live a new life

v 6-7   "We know" that our old self was put away so that sin's influence in us would be nullified

v 8-10   "We know" that the power of Christ's resurrection will also triumph in us

6:11-14 Answer Part Two: No, the gospel gives you power over sin as well

v 11   Though you know you are dead to sin, you must also treat yourself as dead to sin

v 12-13 United with Christ, you can obey sin or obey God, so obey God

v 14   Since you are not under the law anymore, sin's mastery over you is and will be broken

6:15   The second question: Does the gospel (the message you are no longer "under the law") leave you free to live in any way you choose?

6:16-23 Answer Part One: No! You can be either a slave to sin or a servant of God, but no one is free

v 16   Everyone is a slave to something!

v 17-23 There are only two kinds of bond-service: to sin or to God

v 17-18 The origins of each: born into slavery to sin, brought into slavery to God by conversion

v 19   How each develops: slavery to sin results in ever-increasing wickedness; slavery to God leads to holiness v 20-23   The results of each: death (including present brokenness) or eternal life

7:1-6   Answer Part Two: No! You can be either married to the law or married to Christ, but no one is free

v 1-3   Illustration: wives are bound to their husbands until freed by death

v 4-6   Application: we are married to Christ! So we are now (like all married persons) bound with the cords of love, not fear

v 4   How each starts: born into marriage to law; brought into marriage to Christ by his death

v 5-6   The results of each: controlled by sinful nature, leading to death; serving in the way of the Spirit

7:7a   The third question: Is the law a bad thing (since bondage to the law caused evil)?

7:7b-12 Answer: No, it was sin in me that made the law ineffective

v 7b   The law exposes sin for what it is

v 8   Sin is aroused by its exposure to the law

v 9   The law convicts of sin

v 10-11   Thus the law brings both aggravation of sin and overwhelming conviction of guilt

v 12   Summary: the law is good, but I am sinful

7:13a   The fourth question: Is the law a killer?

7:13b   Answer: No, sin is the killer

7:14-25 Our experience of remaining sin (NB v 18-20 recapitulate v 14-17)

v 14/18   Our weakness: we have remaining sinful nature, prone to evil

v 15-16/19 Our inner conflict: sin leads us to do things we hate

v 17/20   Our identity: in a sense then, when we sin, it is the sin in us that does it, not our truest self v 21   Our dilemma: the more we seek to do and be good, the more evil within presses upon us

v 22-23 The two forces of the Christian heart:

Love of God's law in my truest self ("the law of my mind")

Sin that hates the law of God ("law in my members")

v 24-25 The two cries of the Christian heart:

Discouragement: who will rescue me?

Hope: Christ has rescued and will rescue me!

APPENDIX: Identifying the Idols of the Heart

What Idolatry Is

In the book of Romans, Paul develops a profound anatomy of sin. He shows us that sin goes much deeper than mere behavioral violations; it begins at the motivational level. This is why, as he will go on to explain in Romans 8, sin cannot be resisted through mere willpower, but only through the application of gospel truth by the Holy Spirit, at the motivational level.

But in chapters 1 – 7, Paul first has shown us what sin really is, and how sin operates deep under the surface of our lives. This appendix "collects" his teaching on this topic, and combines it with other biblical material, to bring out the fullness of the subject.

So far, Paul has said:

1. Our root problem is our unwillingness to glorify God, to give him the centrality that is his due. "Although they knew God, they neither glorified him as God nor gave thanks to him" (1:21).

2. Therefore, we choose created things to be our "gods." In order to deny God control of our lives, each of us chooses a created thing (or things) to live for and worship instead. We "worshiped … created things rather than the Creator" (1:25). We must worship something.

3. Therefore, each life is distorted by a life lie. At the base of all our life choices, our emotional structure, and our personality is a false belief system centered on an idol—the belief that something besides God can give us the life and joy that only God can give. We have "exchanged the truth of God for a lie" (1:25). We look to something besides Jesus to be our "savior," our "righteousness," the thing that makes us good and acceptable.

4. But each life is a kind of bondage. No one is actually "free," for we must serve whatever it is we have decided to live for—

so people have "worshiped and served created things" (1:25). Since every human being must have an ultimate "good" by which all other choices are made and values are judged, we all "offer [our]selves" to something (6:16). Therefore, every human being is in "covenant service" to a "lord" that works out its will through our bodies (6:16-19).

5. Even after conversion, our old, false saviors/lords and their attendant false belief systems still distort our lives—unless the power of the Holy Spirit continually renews our minds and hearts (7:14-25).

6. The key to freedom is the application of the gospel of grace. "Sin shall not be your master, because you are not under law, but under grace" (6:14).

Here is another way of summarizing the Bible's teaching on idolatry, this time using Genesis 3 (a passage Paul has firmly in mind as he writes Romans 1:18-31 and 5:12-21). We can think about it as six steps:

1. *Pride.* Sin is to seek to be God, self-existent and sovereign over oneself. Sin is a desire to create a secure, independent life apart from God. It's an unwillingness to trust God, to admit we are creatures dependent on him. So the serpent promises Eve: "You will be like God" (Genesis 3:5).

2. *Fear.* Sin-pride leads to a pervasive awareness of our weakness and guilt. Thus there's a drive to get both control and worth while hiding from God, self, and others. "I was afraid ... so I hid" (3:10).

3. *The Lie.* Sin-anxiety moves us to construct an idol-based belief system by which we seek power and worth as independent from God. We trust the idols for these things. The idol system distorts the way we perceive ourselves, success and failure, God, the world, and others. "You will not surely die ... for God knows that when you eat of it your eyes will be opened" (3:4-5).

4. *Self-justification.* The life-lie leads to a life of pleasing the idol(s). Choices and behavior are designed to seek its blessings and avoid its curses. All idol systems are essentially a form of "works righteousness", each with its own set of standards and laws. "They ... made coverings for themselves" (3:7).

5. *Lusts.* Because we give idols power to justify us, we must have them; this creates deep, inordinate drives and desires that master us and can't be controlled. Our idols control us by capturing our imagination in the form of vivid, positive pictures of certain conditions we believe will make us happy and fulfilled. "Your desire will be for your husband, and he will rule over you" (3:16).

6. *Varied miseries.* Depending on what our circumstances are and how our self-justifying efforts go, our pain will differ. If someone or something blocks us from getting what we want, there is anger and scape-goating. If some condition threatens our idols, there is deep fear and anxiety. If we fail our idol significantly, there is despair and self-hatred or guilt. If we please our idol fairly successfully, there is still emptiness and boredom.

Identifying our Idols

Here is a (non-exhaustive) list of idol-based "life-lies:"

Life only has meaning, or I only have worth, if...

... I have power and influence over others. *Power idolatry*

... I am loved and respected by... *Approval idolatry*

... I have this kind of pleasure experience, or this particular quality of life. *Comfort idolatry*

... I have a particular kind of look or body image. *Image idolatry*

... I am able to get mastery over my life in the area of...
Control idolatry

... people are dependent on me and need me. *Helping idolatry*

... someone is there to protect me and keep me safe.
Dependence idolatry

... I am completely free from any obligations or responsibilities to take care of someone. *Independence idolatry*

... I am highly productive, getting a lot done. *Work idolatry*

... I am being recognized for my accomplishments, and/or if I am excelling in my career. *Achievement idolatry*

... I have a certain level of wealth, financial freedom, and very nice possessions. *Materialism idolatry*

... I am adhering to my religion's moral codes and am accomplished in its activities. *Religion idolatry*

... this one person is in my life and happy there and/or happy with me. *Individual person idolatry*

... I feel I am totally independent of organized religion and have a self-made morality. *Irreligion idolatry*

... my race and culture are ascendant and/or recognized in some way as superior. *Racial/cultural idolatry*

... a particular social, professional, or other group lets me in. *Belonging idolatry*

... my children and/or my parents are happy and happy with me. *Family idolatry*

... Mr or Ms "Right" is in love with me. *Relationship idolatry*

... I am hurting or in a problem. Only then do I feel noble, worthy of love, or able to deal with guilt. *Suffering idolatry*

... my political or social cause or party is making progress and ascending in influence or power. *Ideology idolatry*

When we are experiencing negative emotions, we need to find the possible idolatrous sources. For example:

■ If you are angry, ask: *Is there something too important to me? Something I am telling myself I have to have? Is that why I am angry—because I am being blocked from having something I think is a necessity when it is not?"*

■ If you are fearful or badly worried, ask: *Is there something too important to me? Something I am telling myself I have to have? Is that why I am so scared—because something is being threatened which I think is a necessity when it is not?*

■ If you are despondent or hating yourself, ask: *Is there something too important to me? Something I am telling myself I have to have? Is that why I am so "down"—because I have lost or failed at something I think is a necessity when it is not?*

We can therefore get to the root identity of our idols by asking some diagnostic questions:

■ *What is my greatest nightmare? What do I worry about most?*

■ *What, if I failed or lost it, would cause me to feel that I did not even want to live? What keeps me going?*

■ *What do I rely on or comfort myself with when things go bad or get difficult?*

■ *What do I think most easily about? What does my mind go to when I am free? What preoccupies me?*

■ *What prayer, unanswered, would make me seriously think about turning away from God?*

■ *What makes me feel the most self-worth? What am I proudest of?*

■ *What do I really want and expect out of life? What would really make me happy?*

As we answer these questions, common themes may well reveal themselves. We begin to see what things tend to be too important to us: what our "functional" masters seem to be.

Dismantling our Idols

Once we have identified our idols, there are three ways to go about dismantling them.

1. The "moralizing" approach says: *Your problem is that you are sinning here and here. Repent, and stop!* This focuses on behavior, so doesn't go deep enough. We must find out the *why* of behavior—what inordinate desires are working and the idols and false beliefs behind them. Simply to tell an unhappy person to "repent and change your life" won't help because the lack of self-control is coming from a belief that says: *If you don't have this, even if you live up to moral standards, you are still a failure.* You must replace this belief by repenting of the one sin under it all—your particular idolatry.

2. The "psychologizing" approach says: *Your problem is that you don't see that God loves you as you are.* This focuses on feelings, so doesn't go deep enough. We must find out the reason a person doesn't feel happy or loved—what inordinate desires are working and the idols and false beliefs behind them. Simply to tell an unhappy person "God loves you" won't help, because the unhappiness is coming from a belief that says: *If you don't have this, you are still a failure even if God loves you.* You must replace this belief by repenting of the one sin under it all—your particular idolatry.

3. The "gospel application" approach says: *Your problem is that you are looking to something besides Christ to be your happiness.* This confronts a person with the real sin that lies under the sins and behind the bad feelings. Repentance for rejecting Christ's free grace and acceptance is a sorrowful yet joyful act. Paul tells us that the bondage of sin is broken when we come out from under the law. Every idol is the center of some system of works righteousness by which we are seeking to "earn" our salvation by pleasing the idol. Every idol system is a way to be "under the law." Only when we realize we are righteous in Christ is the idol's power over us broken. "Sin shall not be your master, because you are not under law, but under grace" (Romans 6:14). To live and think of yourself

as "under grace" means that no created thing can now master or control you. Instead, you can enjoy them.

Here is how to apply this third approach:

Unmask the idols. We must remember that idols create a "delusional field" around themselves. We have deified them and inflated them cognitively and emotionally. Remember that we have magnified them in our eyes to be more wonderful and all-powerful than they are.

Most of all, remind yourself of what you are saying to God when you pine after idols (in your anger, fear, despondency). You are saying something like this: *Lord, it's good to have you, but there's this other thing I must have, without which life is not happy or meaningful. If I can't have it, I will despair. You are not enough. I need this too, as a requirement for being fulfilled. In fact, if you would take it from me, I'd turn my back on you, for you are negotiable but this is not! This is the real goal of my life—if you are not useful to me in achieving it, I might turn away from you.*

It is important to see what we are really saying and to recognize both the unreasonableness and the cruelty of it. We need to see how ungrateful we are being to Jesus. And we need to see how, at bottom, this is another way of avoiding Jesus as Savior, and trying to be our own.

Repent of this sin beneath all other sins. This has to happen in two stages:

- Hating the sin for itself. *Lord, I see how repulsive this thing is as an idol. Lord, the thing itself is not evil—it is what my heart has done to it, elevating it, that makes it evil. I refuse to be controlled by it any longer. It wreaks havoc in my life. You justify me, not this. You are my master, not this. I will not be controlled by this. This is not my life—I don't have to have it. Christ is my life—I only have to have him.*

- Rejoicing in the grace and work of Jesus. *Lord, I have been trying to earn my own salvation and weave my own righteousness. But you are my salvation and righteousness. I am accepted in your Son! All my problems come because I am forgetting how loved, honored, beautiful, secure, rich, respected, embraced, and free in Jesus I am. All other ways of finding honor, respect, purpose, and so on are vain. Let me be so ravished with your love for me that no other love can control me.*

APPENDIX: The Recent Debate

Recently a "new perspective" has developed over what the term "observing the law" (or, as the ESV puts it, "works of the law") means in Romans 3:20, 28.

Many interpreters believe Paul is talking about the Mosaic ceremonial law only—circumcision, the dietary laws, and the other laws which are about keeping ritually "clean." In this view, "works of the law" is not moral performance in general, but the adoption of Jewish cultural customs and ethnic boundary markers. Paul is not therefore addressing, and countering, a works-righteousness system of salvation (ie: the idea that you must obey particular laws in order to be right with God). Instead, the argument goes, Paul is opposing a view that Gentile Christians must take on Jewish ethnic markers and become culturally Jewish.

So in this "new perspective" the Jews to whom Paul is speaking in Romans 2 and 3 are not legalists, but nationalists. And Paul is therefore not opposing salvation-by-works, but rather, racial and ethnic exclusivity. This means that Paul's purpose in the book of Romans is to insist that all races and classes sit down equally at the "table of God," because we are all one in Christ.

I have taken extensive time to weigh the pros and cons of this "new perspective," and I believe it is very helpful in several ways, but that it cannot overthrow the essence of the historic, classic approach. This is not the place for an in-depth analysis, and what follows is certainly not intended to be any sort of last word, but here are my brief conclusions...

You cannot ultimately drive a wedge between nationalism and legalism as if they are two separate things. Works of the law probably does include the observance of cultural boundary markers (eg: a reliance on circumcision, 2:25-29; 4:9-12). And this was clearly a serious issue among the Galatian believers, too, with the potential to split that church and undermine the gospel (Galatians 2:1-16). But nationalism is a form of legalism. Legalism is adding anything to Jesus Christ as a requirement for full acceptance with God. A moral superiority that comes from good works or from racial and cultural pedigree grows out of the same spiritual root. The gospel is that we are saved through what Christ does, and not by what we do or are. So when Jews thought that their cultural identity and norms—their Jewishness—saved them, they were adopting a form of self-salvation. Human achievement was becoming the basis for their standing with God.

It is key that Paul associates the works of the law with "boasting" (Romans 3:27-28). And throughout the Scriptures, "boasting" is used about what you rely on and have pride in (see Jeremiah 9:23-24; 1 Corinthians 1:31). Paul says that boasting in, or trusting in, yourself is what underlies the works of the law. So while works of the law can mean relying on (or boasting in) nationalism, it cannot only mean that; nationalism is a form of self-salvation, or legalism. And it is this that Paul means by the phrase "works of the law."

So, ultimately, we must still read the book of Romans as Paul's defense of the gospel of free grace against winning God's favor by human accomplishment or status. The new perspective can't dislodge the classic understanding of Romans. But this debate over the term "works of the law" is nonetheless helpful to us in two ways.

First, it shows us how subtly the gospel can be undermined from within the Christian church and community. The new perspective shows us that those who "called [themselves] a Jew" (Romans 2:17) were not full-bore legalists who flatly rejected Christ.

Instead, they were saying: *Jesus is critical and crucial to getting saved, of course, but faith in him alone is not enough for full acceptance with God. We must continue to perform the full range of Mosaic ceremonial and cultural customs.* This is much more subtle.

In the same way, spirit-deadening moralism would not grow in our churches by blatant, obvious denials of the doctrine of justification by faith alone. This truth is much more likely to be undermined in new forms of demanding cultural conformity or other approaches, which are much more subtle.

Second, this debate shows us that the book of Romans has often been read too much as a rather academic debate about doctrine. But Paul is not only, or mainly, concerned about a breakdown in the doctrinal beliefs of individuals. He has a deep concern about a breakdown in Christian unity and community. It is important to see how much the book of Romans is addressed to the problems of how people from very different cultural backgrounds and religious traditions can live in unity as Christians. The truths of the gospel are not matters only for the ivory tower, for lecture rooms and doctoral theses; they are fundamental to everyday life, in the heart and the home, with congregation members and co-workers.

BIBLIOGRAPHY

■ Augustine, *Confessions* (Mentor/Penguin, 1963)

■ Greg Bahnsen, *Presuppositional Apologetics Stated and Defended* (American Vision, 2010)

■ William Barclay, *Great Themes of the New Testament* (Westminster John Knox Press, 2001)

■ John Calvin, *Commentaries on the Epistle of Paul to the Romans,* translated by John Owen (Calvin Translation Society, 1849)

■ John H. Gerstner, *Theology for Everyman* (Moody Press, 1965)

■ William Guthrie, *The Christian's Great Interest* (Banner of Truth, 1969)

■ Charles Hodge, *Princeton Sermons* (Thomas Nelson & Sons, 1879)

■ D. James Kennedy, *Evangelism Explosion* (Tyndale House, 1973)

■ C.S. Lewis, *Mere Christianity* (Macmillan, 1969)

■ D. Martyn Lloyd-Jones, *Romans Series* (Zondervan, 1989)

■ Richard Lovelace, *Dynamics of Spiritual Life* (IVP, 1979)

■ Martin Luther, *Commentary on the Epistle to the Romans* (Kregel Classics, 2003)

■ Rebecca Manley Pippert, *Out of the Saltshaker and into the World: Evangelism as a Way of Life* (IVP, 1999)

■ Douglas J. Moo, *The Epistle to the Romans* in The New International Commentary Series (Eerdmans, 1996)

■ John Murray, *The Atonement* (Baker Book House, 1962)

- John Murray, *The Epistle to the Romans* (Zondervan, 1959)

- John Owen, "On the Mortification of Sin in Believers" in *Temptation and Sin* (Zondervan, 1958)

- Blaise Pascal, "Pensées" in *The Works of Pascal* (Random House, 1941)

- John Piper, The Roots of Endurance (Crossway, 2002)

- J.C. Ryle, *The Select Sermons of George Whitefield with an Account of his Life* (Banner of Truth Trust, 1990)

- Richard Sibbes, *The Work of Richard Sibbes, volume V* (Nicol Edition, now published BiblioBazaar—first published in this edition 1923)

- John Stott, *Men Made New* (IVP, 1966)

- John Stott, *The Message of Romans* in the Bible Speaks Today series (IVP Academic, 2001)

Romans 1 – 7 for...
Bible-study Groups

Timothy Keller's **Good Book Guide** to Romans 1–7 is the companion to this resource, helping groups of Christians to explore, discuss and apply the book together. Seven studies, each including investigation, apply, getting personal, pray and explore more sections, take you through the first seven chapters of Romans. Includes a concise Leader's Guide at the back.

Find out more at:
www.thegoodbook.com/goodbookguides

Daily Devotionals

Explore daily devotional helps you open up the Scriptures and will encourage and equip you in your walk with God. Available as a quarterly booklet, *Explore* is also available as an app, where you can download Dr Keller's notes on Romans and other books of the Bible, alongside contributions from trusted Bible teachers including Mark Dever, Stephen Um, Albert Mohler, Sam Allberry, and Juan Sanchez.

Find out more at:
www.thegoodbook.com/explore

The Whole Series

- **Exodus For You** *Tim Chester*

- **Judges For You** *Timothy Keller*

- **Ruth For You** *Tony Merida*

- **1 Samuel For You** *Tim Chester*

- **2 Samuel For You** *Tim Chester*

- **Nehemiah For You** *Eric Mason*

- **Psalms For You** *Christopher Ash*

- **Proverbs For You** *Kathleen Nielson*

- **Isaiah For You** *Tim Chester*

- **Daniel For You** *David Helm*

- **Micah For You** *Stephen Um*

- **Mark For You** *Jason Meyer*

- **Luke 1-12 For You** *Mike McKinley*

- **Luke 12-24 For You** *Mike McKinley*

- **John 1-12 For You** *Josh Moody*

- **John 13-21 For You** *Josh Moody*

- **Acts 1-12 For You** *Albert Mohler*

- **Acts 13-28 For You** *Albert Mohler*

- **Romans 1-7 For You** *Timothy Keller*

- **Romans 8-16 For You** *Timothy Keller*

- **1 Corinthians For You** *Andrew Wilson*

- **2 Corinthians For You** *Gary Millar*

- **Galatians For You** *Timothy Keller*

- **Ephesians For You** *Richard Coekin*

- **Philippians For You** *Steven Lawson*

- **Colossians & Philemon For You**
  Mark Meynell

- **1 & 2 Timothy For You** *Phillip Jensen*

- **Titus For You** *Tim Chester*

- **Hebrews For You** *Michael Kruger*

- **James For You** *Sam Allberry*

- **1 Peter For You** *Juan Sanchez*

- **2 Peter & Jude For You** *Miguel Núñez*

- **Revelation For You** *Tim Chester*

Find out more about these resources at:
www.thegoodbook.com/for-you
www.thegoodbook.co.uk/for-you

Good Book Guides
The full range

thegoodbook

COMPANY

BIBLICAL | RELEVANT | ACCESSIBLE

At The Good Book Company, we are dedicated to helping Christians and local churches grow. We believe that God's growth process always starts with hearing clearly what he has said to us through his timeless word—the Bible.

Ever since we opened our doors in 1991, we have been striving to produce Bible-based resources that bring glory to God. We have grown to become an international provider of user-friendly resources to the Christian community, with believers of all backgrounds and denominations using our books, Bible studies, devotionals, evangelistic resources, and DVD-based courses.

We want to equip ordinary Christians to live for Christ day by day, and churches to grow in their knowledge of God, their love for one another, and the effectiveness of their outreach.

Call us for a discussion of your needs or visit one of our local websites for more information on the resources and services we provide.

Your friends at The Good Book Company

thegoodbook.com | thegoodbook.co.uk
thegoodbook.com.au | thegoodbook.co.nz
thegoodbook.co.in